The
Really Lancashire
BOOK

Edited by
Bob Dobson

Landy Publishing
1997

ISBN 1 872895 36 0

British Library Cataloguing in Publication Data.
A catalogue record for this book is available from the British Library

Landy Publishing have also published:-

A Lancashire Look by Benita Moore
A Blackburn Miscellany by Bob Dobson
Bits of Old Blackburn by J. G. Shaw & William Hulme
Accrington Observed by Bob Dobson & Brian Brindle
Accrington's Changing Face by Frank Watson & Bob Dobson
An Accrington Mixture edited by Bob Dobson
Blackburn's Shops at the Turn of the Century by Matthew Cole
Blackburn's West End by Matthew Cole
Policing Wigan by James Fairhurst
Warton & Freckleton Recalled by Peter Benson
Threads of Lancashire Life by Winnie Bridges

A full list of publications is available from:
Landy Publishing, 'Acorns', 3 Staining Drive, Staining, Blackpool FY3 0BU
Tel & fax: 01253 895678

FOREWORD (Forrad)

This book came about as a result of me having to finish publishing a magazine called **REALLY LANCASHIRE**; a magazine for the Red Rose County. After four issues, May 1995 to February 1996, I couldn't make it pay, so swallowed my pride and called it a day.

It was a magazine for the Red Rose County, and contained a mixture of material, edited by me, which seemed to find favour with its readers. So, having some material left over, and not being able to stop looking at Lancashire-related stuff I could make a story out of, I decided to compile this book and offer it to those who had subscribed to **REALLY LANCASHIRE**, to those who have in the past bought my publications from me, and to the Lancashire public through bookshops.

The result is in your hands. It is a mixture, a hot-pot, of all sorts of written matter of some Lancashire interest, seasoned with pictures of one sort or another.

By "*Lancashire*" I mean the traditional county whose boundaries got mucked about with by the administrators and politicians in 1974. Let it be clearly understood - there's no such county as Merseyside or Greater Manchester. There's only one county the Queen is Duke of - **LANCASHIRE**, as defined by Common Usage since Godknowswhen, and unable to be destroyed, be it by politicians or t'Post Office.

History, literature, humour, dialect and much more besides, are here by the bucketful. There's nowt on Yorkshire. My intention is that when you have read it, you'll say - "*That's really Lancashire*".

I thank those who have contributed their work for little reward to help make this an interesting, varied book. Additionally I thank the librarians I have consulted in the past year or so and who have consistently been a source of knowledge or provided the wherewithal to find the information I sought. My friends Mike Clarke, Gerry Wolstenholme and June Huntingdon also deserve my special thanks for their support. So too does my wife, Peggie, for hers.

I apologise to those people whose work I have in my files and can't use. I am already looking forward to the possibility of publishing, in late 1998 hopefully, **THE REALLY LANCASHIRE BOOK No.2**.

Bob Dobson

August 1997

CONTENTS.

Michael May does, with all his might, extoll the virtues of

LANCASHIRE

Its 'ed a deal o' moither, this Cahnty Palatine of eawrs.
Its bin fowt in, fowt o'er, plundered, an' its sin its share o' wars.
Bud th'essence o' these 'appenin's is wod med us wod wi ar,
Thi've composted in its 'istry's soil an' browt us aw to fleawr.

Its browt up mony an 'eroe, ay an' mony a villain too,
An' its sired sum o' t' Royalty, an' bred a King er two,
An' t' spirit o' wod 'appened to 'em, er wod thi browt t' pass,
Is i' th' 'earts thats beatin' in each Lanky lad an' lass.

Its browt up plain an' fancy fooak, like its tradesmen an' its squires,
Bud it's famous fer its experts that warn't fon in other Shires,
Thi wer t' weyvers in its mills, i' t' days of Owd King Cotton,
An' 'appen thers nooan nahadays, bud thi'll never bi fergotton.

Wi've cleyned it up a bit nah, an' weshed its sooty face,
An' thi' 'ardly look t' same features frae its cotton factry days,
Bud it warn't aw muck an' chimneys, even in its days o' yore,
Wi've allus 'ed green 'ills an' fells, an' miles o' rollin' moor.

Wi've geet eawr streams an' rivers, flashin' an' splashin' dahn to t' sea,
An' miles an' miles o' sandy shore, wi' its seabirds wild an' free,
An' acre upon acre o' fields of ooats an' corn,
As ripple wen th' wind blows, like gowden seawaves in a storm.

Wi've geet eawr way o' talkin', wi' dialect in eawr speech,
An' wi 'ed eawr way o' walkin' wen wi'd clogs on aw eawr feet,
Even tho' ther nod as common nah, thi'll never quite dee aht,
As long as born an' bred Lancastrians ar abaht.

Ay, mon! 'Ere wi've getten it aw, Ah wouldn't swop an inch,
Fer t' rest o' t' world together, neauw, nod even fer a pinch!
Thers places 'ere thats nicer than i' Cornwall er i' Devon,
An' i' this shop Ah'll allus stop: Its mi little bit of 'Eaven.

A general view of Greenberfield Locks

The first lock-keeper at Greenberfield was a retired Army Officer named Isaac Jones. In 1824 on the occasion of the opening of the three separate locks his son erected a sun dial on the side of the cottage. It is still there to-day, making the cottage the only one on the canal system to sport such a contrivance.

Greenberfield has hardly changed since 1824. It is at once remote and accessible - being only two miles from Barnoldswick. No better spot could be found for an interesting and relaxing picnic lunch.

CLITHEROE.

Firm on a rock stands this old country town,
Its castle through ages to us has come down,
And proudly old Clitheroe wears her grey crown,
    At the foot of Pendle Hill.

Oft on the walls of the old tower I stand,
Entranced with the beauties that gem the land ;
For Nature has gracefully waved her wand
    At the foot of Pendle Hill.

Charmed with the sight strange emotions have I felt ;
Villages surround it like a jewelled belt,
While the town itself in modesty is knelt
    At the foot of Pendle Hill.

Pleasant are the streams that wander through its vales,
Pleasing to me are the legendary tales ;
Whose birthplace is in these romantic dales
    At the foot of Pendle Hill.

Still in these vales many fair witches dwell,
That throw their enchantments o'er every dell,
From the purple heights of Waddington fell
    To the foot of Pendle Hill.

Clitheroe.   ROBERT HANSON.

9

A Dedicated Amateur: W W Parr of Blackpool F C

In the days before all footballers became simply 'players', William Wilfred Parr was an amateur playing for a professional club. He had started playing in the Fylde Wednesday League. Blackpool were alerted as to his potential; they watched him for a couple of games and invited him to Bloomfield Road in the early part of the 1934/35 season.

A welcome was extended to him at the club by the manager Joe Smith, who invited him to play for the club as an amateur, training on the ground whenever it was possible. Billy had always fitted his football in around his job as a clerk in the Blackpool Corporation Cleansing Department offices and so it was no easy decision for him to commit himself to a professional club. Billy wrote confirming that he was prepared to give it a try. He played a few Northern Mid-Week League games, the equivalent of "A" team matches, and was then thrust into the Central League side, aged 18, against Sheffield United at Bramall Lane on 17th November where his inside forward partner was the great Jimmy Hampson, whose career was in the doldrums. He was officially still on trial but impressed sufficiently with his *'excellent work on the wing'* in a 3-0 win for Joe Smith to register him as an amateur for the remainder of the season.

Even though he was on the books of a professional club, Billy Parr was still only being given time off by his employers providing that he made it up from his holidays; in addition Blackpool had to take out an insurance at a premium of two pounds per annum, to indemnify the Corporation in the event of Parr being injured. Parr's true loyalties were with his office but, despite the clash of interests and difficulties with his employers, Parr played in 26 of the final 30 Reserves' games of the season. He signed amateur forms for the 1935/36 season and played for the Reds (possibles) against the Stripes (probables) in pre-season practice matches where his partnership with a young George Eastham for the Reds in the opening game *"was one of the highlights of a game which had few of them"*. He started the League season in the Reserves but an injury to Dick Watmough in the opening Second Division game saw Parr withdrawn from the Reserves so that he could make his first team debut against Norwich City.

An Office Boy on a Man's Errand

Blackpool won 2-1 and Parr, right wing in one of Blackpool's youngest-ever forward lines, did not disgrace himself. He retained his place for the next five games and when he scored one of the goals in the 4-1 win over West Ham United, he was the first Blackpool amateur to score a first team goal since before World War 1. After two further games, Watmough returned to the side and Parr was back in the Reserves. He played six further games towards the end of the season and, despite offers to turn professional, remained an amateur.

His early season form had caught the eye of the amateur selectors and he was invited to play for Lancashire against Staffordshire on 11th January 1936 and in an amateur international trial, North versus South at Ilford on 18th January. His performance impressed the England amateur selectors who chose him to play against Wales. The game was cancelled due to the death of King George V, so Parr and the other players were named for the next international against Ireland on 15th February at Middlesborough. The game was switched to Blackpool, as Middlesborough were involved in a Cup tie, so Billy made his international debut in front of his home crowd. England won 5-0 and the 3,000 spectators, delighted to see a home town boy playing at international level, cheered every time Parr touched the ball.

An International in the 'A' Team

The following week Billy Parr found himself back playing with Blackpool - in the "A" team. He did not play for Blackpool again until late in the season but he did play in the two other home internationals for the England amateurs.

Joe Smith tried to get Parr to re-sign as an amateur in June 1936 but Billy reported he was unable to do so, because of work commitments. Because the situation caused him a problem he even considered retiring from the game. This prompted the Blackpool chairman Mr. Parkinson to speak to Mr. Entwistle, the Cleaning Superintendent, with a view to Parr being released to play and to train one afternoon and two evenings each week. A compromise was reached, Parr could play *'when required'* and would be allowed to train one morning per week; he re-signed in late August much to the relief of Joe Smith who had only one other right winger, Watmough, on the books.

Parr started the 1936/37 season in the Reserves but injury to Watmough saw him back in the first team for the third game, after work prevented him playing in the second. Blackpool saw this as a problem and, after discussion in the Board room, the club wrote to the chairman of the Cleansing Committee, requesting Parr's leave of absence for football. He stayed in the side for four games before returning to the Reserves and playing regularly for Lancashire. He had the satisfaction of playing in the side in a season that they won promotion to the First Division.

In January 1937 he was approached to tour New Zealand and Australia with an FA Amateur XI in the close season and whilst Blackpool gave their permission, it took another approach to the Town Hall to release Parr for the tour. Parr thanked the club for their assistance before going off to play for England against Wales on 23rd January. He scored in a resounding 9-1 success but the side fared less well in a 5-1 defeat by Ireland in February. This cost him, and seven others, their places for the forthcoming Scotland game.

In March, Parr asked Blackpool to be excused for the rest of the season in view of the fact that he had a long overseas tour approaching which would necessitate him being away from his office. Blackpool were loathe to lose his services and Joe Smith persuaded him to play on until after the Easter fixtures. Once they were over, he devoted himself to his work prior to setting off for New Zealand in May. The tour was classified as an Empire tour and included amongst the players Bernard Joy, who had played in Parr's first three internationals, with whom he was to form a firm friendship.

The team played in Colombo before they started the New Zealand leg of the tour. This went well and Parr scored in the opening

11

fixture. The remaining eight games were all won with a goal aggregate of 85 for and just six against: Parr scored six goals, including two against New Zealand. In Australia four games were played and whilst three of them were won, the match against Australia at Sydney was lost 5-4 and an Empire side suffered its first defeat in 93 games on tour.

For the 1937/38 season, Parr did not want to sign amateur forms until the club had made satisfactory arrangements with the Cleansing Committee for his release. To this end, a Blackpool director, Councillor Singleton, spoke to Mr. Furness who pointed out that Parr had *"already had a long leave of absence for football purposes"* and it was thought desirable that he *"should devote more time to his work"*. The situation was left that *"should Parr be required urgently at any time permission would be given for his release"*.

Although he played no first team games in the 1937/38 season, mainly because of representative commitments, he did turn out occasionally for the Reserves. He also played in the three England Amateur internationals and he had his best day against Wales at Rhyl in January 1938 when he scored four in an 8-2 win. In addition there was a 1-1 draw with Ireland and a satisfying 5-2 win over Scotland in March which was his last international as a Blackpool player.

Parr agreed to sign amateur forms for the 1938/39 season and played regularly with the Reserves until an unexpected call up for the first team against Preston North End on 29th October 1938 when the forward line was re-shuffled because of injury. It was to be Parr's only game in the First Division and the local press headlined him as one of the *"Bright Spots"* of the game and followed this with *"Parr's game was at one time a revelation, he can centre from every possible and impossible angle"*. Despite this praise he played no more first team football at Blackpool.

To London

In November 1938 Blackpool reluctantly cancelled his registration when he took up a promotion in the Wembley Council offices. Millwall were immediately interested in signing him but Parr opted for the amateur game with Dulwich Hamlet and it was from there that he won his ninth amateur cap. He had missed the first two internationals of the season but was back for the Scotland game in March 1939 and scored two in England's 8-3 win. It was his final international. Both his first and last were played in front of his home team crowd. Billy often returned to Blackpool to visit his parents. On one such occasion, Blackpool arranged for him to visit Bloomfield Road where, before the Good Friday game with Arsenal in 1939, he was presented with a gold wrist watch in thanks for his services to the club.

When war broke out he enlisted with the RAF, despite being in a reserved occupation. Before he took up active service, he played a single game for Arsenal in 1939/40, through his friendship with Bernard Joy, and a number for Wealdstone, all as a guest player. Sadly Sergeant-Pilot Parr was declared "killed on active service" on 10th March 1942, aged just 26 when he crashed during an RAF night flight, ironically at the same time as younger brother Ron was reported missing following the fall of Singapore. It was a sad loss to his family and the football world. The mourners were many when he was buried in Marton cemetery, Blackpool. Probably the most fitting tribute came from Blackpool manager Joe Smith who said *"If he had made football his profession he would have been one of the greatest players in the land. He was a gentleman - every inch of him - on and off the field"*.

Yar Nell

by Hazel Clegg

Neaw, id wer durin' t' Thirties,
Un t' Cotton Trade wer bad.
Yar Nell ud bin med redundant,
Hoo warn'd 'alf 'oppin' mad.

But hoo geet a job ut Blackpoo',
Away fro' t' weyvin' shed,
Un t' loom, un t' weft, un t' shuttle,
- Un nine t' five i' stead.

Mam rigs Nell eawt reet gradely,
New frock, new coat, new hat,
Suede shoon, un' fine silk stockin's,
Lace undercloas, vest un' brat.

Wi sis Nell off ut t' station,
Mi heart fur bust wi pride,
Hoo wer doin' her bit fer t' nation,
Ay mon, Ah cud uh cried.

Wi goes on t' chara t' Blackpoo',
'Caus it cum Whitsun Tide,
To si Yar Nell, thad aw wer well,
Un' to give har a reet surprise.

Nell's digs wer whoam fro' whoam,
T'landlady be a Missus O'Shea,
Stout legs, un' ample busum,
Med 'Hot Pot' fur uz tay.

Wi bout sum rock fur t' chilther,
Un walks up 'Mile o' Gowd',
Then on t' Pier,
Thowt wid 'ave uz fortunes towd.

Wey, Ah fur gawps at t'fortune teller,
Uz sez, "Nay, Ah'll go to 'ell",
'Caus, t'gypsy on t'North Pier,
Nobbut war - **Yar Nell**!

13

David Pickup tells with pride of

LANCASHIRE'S MORMON CONNECTIONS

Mention the name Mormon and many will recall the world-famous Mormon Tabernacle Choir, the Osmonds singing group, or perhaps that the Church has its headquarters in Salt Lake City, Utah. People will also associate the Mormons with the building of awe-inspiring religious edifices of great beauty. As a Mormon temple has been constructed in the heart of Lancashire, in full view of the M61 motorway on the northern outskirts of Chorley, people are asking *"Who are the Mormons and why have they built a temple in Lancashire?"* To answer this question, one needs to have some understanding of the significance of Lancashire for the Mormons.

To most people, 'Mormon' suggests an American religion. Many will have met the smartly dressed young missionaries of the Church, some with North American accents. Today the largest concentration of members of the **Church of Jesus Christ of Latter-day Saints**, nicknamed the Mormons, is found in Canada and the United States, where the Church is the fastest growing religion. It is not surprising that the Church is often seen as American.

The truth is not only that Mormons are part of an over ten million strong world-wide Church, with only about half of its members within the United States, but that a very significant proportion of the 'American' members are in fact descendants of nineteenth century British converts, many from Lancashire!

The Church of Jesus Christ of Latter-day Saints was formally organised on 6th April 1830. Within a few short years, by 1837, missionaries had arrived in England at Liverpool and found a welcome reception to their preaching from the people of Lancashire, who flocked to join the Church. Branches were rapidly established in almost every town and village along the Ribble Valley and from Preston through the villages down to Chorley. With this firm foothold in the Preston area, the missionary work soon spread to other parts of Britain. Within eight months of the arrival of just seven missionaries on 19th July 1837, membership had reached 2,000. In some cases whole villages joined the Mormons; in many others at least half the inhabitants were converted. Although that early success was to continue throughout the nineteenth century, by the turn of the century Mormonism had all but vanished from Britain.

In June 1863, Charles Dickens went on board the passenger ship Amazon, bound for New York, to report on an unusual phenomenon: the organised emigration of many thousands of British Mormons to strengthen their fledgling Church in the American West. *"I went on board their ship to bear testimony against them if they deserved it, as I fully believed they would: to my great astonishment they did not deserve it."* Dickens was surprised by what he found. He wrote that not knowing who they were he would have described the English Mormons *"…in their degree, the pick and flower of England."*

Between 6th June 1840, the date of the first sailing from Liverpool of 41 saints, as members of the Mormon Church are called, and 1870, some 45,000 emigrated to North America. During the same period converts to the Church in this country totalled 100,000. Emigration was actively encouraged. For some 50 years from 1840 the Church in America was predominantly British. The new members were needed to build up the young Church going through a period of bitter persecution that was eventually to force them to leave Illinois for land previously unsettled in the Rocky Mountains in the west. A very large proportion of the Mormon pioneers crossing the plains with their handcarts or covered wagons were English, many of them ordinary folk from Lancashire!

Had those converts, and those many thousands that followed until the policy of emigration ceased in the 1950s, remained in this country they could by today have represented a British Church membership of 1,500,000 or more. By the very fact that so many of the Mormon converts emigrated, until fairly recent times Mormons were largely unknown by the population of England, once the tide of emigration had ceased and the marvel of the acceptance of Mormon teaching by so many thousand Lancashire folk having passed beyond living memory.

It is quite possible that, without the influx of British converts, the Mormon Church would not have survived the period of intense persecution in the 1840s. More interestingly, with the remarkable acceptance of the teachings of the Church by the people of this country, particularly in Lancashire, the Mormon Church could easily have become a distinctly British church, with its headquarters not in Salt Lake City, but Preston. Even today, the oldest continuous branch of the Church is in Preston.

Preston was the first location of the preaching of the Mormon faith east of the Atlantic. They arrived on 22nd July 1837, at the height of the election called on the accession to the throne of the eighteen-year-old Queen Victoria. The missionaries were at once invited to preach in the Reverend James Fielding's Vauxhall Chapel, from which congregation the first converts were drawn, seven of whom were baptised in the River Ribble, near the Old Tram Bridge, on Sunday 30th July, before a crowd of some 7,000 Prestonians. Missionaries frequently preached from the steps of the Obelisk in Preston's Market Place and within a few weeks there were five branches of the Church in Preston. Later in the year, the Mormons rented the Cockpit, the former home of Preston's Temperance Movement, for their Sunday services and held a conference of 300 members there on Christmas Day 1837.

In the circumstances of today's increasing British membership of the Church, it is perhaps not at all surprising that a Mormon temple, one of only 60 in the world and only the second in Great Britain, is to be erected in the vicinity of the Church's English roots in Preston. Such a construction would certainly be a fitting tribute to the zeal of those early missionaries, the fruit of whose labours preserved the life-blood of the Mormon Church, and whose influence and effect is felt in the Mormon Church in Britain over 150 years later.

The Mormon's story is not just the story of the success of a new religion but a fascinating insight into a neglected aspect of the social history of Victorian Lancashire.

David Pickup is the author of *The Pick & Flower of England, the Illustrated Story of the Mormons in Victorian England* and *The Story of the Preston Temple*, ISBN 1 874129 01 0, which may be obtained from bookshops at £10.95, or direct from the publishers, Living Legend, 252 Manchester Road, Burnley, BB11 4HF at £12.90, to include post and packing.

THE REMARKABLE MRS. RAFFALD

19th April 1981 was the Bi-centenary of the death of Elizabeth Raffald, cook and author. She was highly intelligent, astute, strong-willed and very diplomatic. Yet few people know of her talents and achievements. She was born in Doncaster in 1733, the daughter of Joshua Whitaker, who was probably a grocer or innkeeper. Elizabeth had a good education including French. She showed a talent for catering and from 1748 until 1763 she was house-keeper in the service of several families. Her last employer was Lady Elizabeth Warburton of Arley Hall, Cheshire, daughter of the Earl of Derby and herself an excellent cook. The family moved in the best society and entertained a great deal, their catering and hospitality of the highest standard.

Young Elizabeth fell in love with the head gardener, John Raffald, a very able botanist and seedsman, whose family came from Stockport. Elizabeth and John were married on 3rd March 1763. After the wedding Mrs. Raffald rented a shop in Fennel Street, Manchester, and opened up as a confectioner. John and his brothers set up a stall in the market place. She took in pupils to learn cookery and domestic economy. They were the daughters of the principal local families. They worked in the kitchens and received lessons in cooking and confectionery, were taught how to pluck poultry, skin hares and to cook and carve joints and game for the table.

Enterprising Elizabeth

There was a large cellar under the premises, which Mrs. Raffald opened as a Servants Agency, the first of its kind. She soon left Fennel Street, but kept the agency on, and took another confectioner's shop at the corner of the Old Exchange Alley, taking her pupils with her. She was an enterprising woman and became celebrated for her supervision of public banquets and private dinners. During this period she was collecting recipes for a book of cookery. In 1769 she published her *'Experienced Housekeeper'* with over 900 recipes, all original and based on practical experience. It was dedicated to Lady Elizabeth Warburton. Constantly pregnant, she had a husband with intemperate habits. When he threatened suicide, she told him to get on with it, so he promptly changed his mind and never mentioned it again!

Publican and Publisher

Mrs. Raffald became the licensee of the *'Bull's Head'* in the Shambles, Market Street, using the bar as her office. Under the same roof she opened and managed Manchester's first Post Office. The *'Experienced Housekeeper'* went into thirteen editions between 1769 and 1806. She sold the copyright to a London publisher in 1773 for £1,400 and there were at least twenty-three pirated editions of the book. It appears that no well-run household was without a copy.

Her efficiency so impressed the officers of the Manchester-based regiments that they had their mess table at the *'Bull's Head'* and followed her later to the *'King's Head'* in Salford. When Elizabeth moved to the King's Head, she compiled and published the first Trades Directory of Manchester and Salford, a volume of some sixty pages. It was issued before the coming of the house-numbering system, and some of the addresses were rather vague, such as *'Top of Salford'*, *'By St.Paul's Chapel'*, *'Top of Longsight'*, *'By Salford Chapel'*, *'By Saracen's Head'*, *'Top of Long Millgate'*. This type of address occupied forty-six pages, each containing an average of thirty-three names. Five pages were filled with an alphabetical list of the country tradesmen, with their warehouses in Manchester, followed by a list of the officers of the Infirmary and Lunatic Hospital. There is an alphabetical list of the Crofters and Bleachers and particulars concerning the stage coach and wagons starting from the town; also a list of the vessels to and from Liverpool on the Old Navigation and the Duke of Bridgewater's vessels; a note as to the Manchester Bank and Insurance Office, also the names of the Justices of the Peace in and near Manchester, seven in number; the names and addresses of the Committee for the Detention and Prosecution of Felons and Receivers of Stolen and Embezzled Goods. It is a very interesting volume and a study of the contents provides a glimpse of the thriving town. The third edition appeared in 1781, the year of Mrs. Raffald's death.

More Courses

A further venture of our heroine was on 4th July 1780 following a public announcement. *'The Ladies Stand on Kersal Moor will be opened on Wednesday next for the accommodation of Ladies and Gentlemen of the town and neighbourhood of Manchester where coffee, tea and chocolate, strawberries and cream will be provided every Wednesday and Friday during the strawberry season, by the public's most obliged and humble servant, Elizabeth Raffald'.*

Kersal Moor was a popular resort for Manchester people and for many years races took place there. It was also the scene of pleasant excursions during the summer months, and this fact would account for Mrs. Raffald making the venture referred to. This was done only the one year and no one knows the results, as she died the following year.

Ghostbuster

Another episode in Elizabeth's life was an experience with her sister in dealing with a ghost. The two were left a house by a relative, and this was reputed to be haunted, so they both travelled to Doncaster to solve the problem. As the tenants went to bed they were disturbed by the ghost who ran into the room, pulled back the curtains and waved some papers in the face of whoever was in the bed. Elizabeth and her sister spent the night in the haunted room, the ghost duly appeared, and was asked by Elizabeth *"In the name of the Father and the Holy Ghost, Who art thou. Where Cam'st thou and what wantest thou?"* The ghost vanished, and was never heard of again, and the house was let assuring a good income for the sisters. Years later, when the house was demolished, human remains were found in the foundations.

In addition to the work already mentioned, Elizabeth was writing a book on midwifery, but this was never published. She died of what were described as *'Spasams'* at the birth of her sixteenth child. Only three of her sixteen daughters survived her and she was buried in Stockport Parish Church in the grave of her husband's family at seven o'clock in the morning. Her name is not on the headstone.

Raffald's Recipes

Her recipes are remarkable, with several methods of cooking each dish. One of her recipes for tart pastry consists of flour, boiling cream and butter, no liquid to bind the mixture: what a rich pastry. She made wines from trees and shrubs in the garden, also pickles, and was keenly interested in herbs for remedies that she dispensed to the poor. The destitute of Manchester and Salford came to her for free medicine and comforts. She was a benefactress to many poor families.

Elizabeth Raffald worked against tremendous odds. Her strength and character rose above the injustices of the time, and set an example to the working women of the period.

Questions and Answers:
Readers questions answered by the Editor

In Swinton there is a legend of a horse and rider falling down a coalmine shaft and living to tell the tale. Is there any truth in this?

In January 1790, Richard Withington, 21 years, of Pendleton was hunting with Squire Hulton of Hulton Park when his horse, with him aboard, fell down a ninety-feet deep mine shaft. The nag was killed, but somehow Richard was saved and rescued by colliers in the Duke of Bridgewater's mine. An inscribed monument was made, though it was probably not erected. This incident, or perhaps one with which it is confused, is recorded briefly in a book by the late Frank Mullineux. In this other incident, a grazing horse fell down a shaft, landed in the aforementioned Duke's underground canal, and walked out none the worse.

A vicar of Bardsley, near Oldham, was a novelist. What was his name?

This was probably Rev. T. P. Wilson, who, at the turn of the century, won a national competition for 'best novel' and got it published. The title was *'Frank Oldfield, or Lost and Found'*. It was a moralistic tale, of 408 pages, set in a South Lancashire mining area, which Bardsley was at that time. A pub opposite Rev. Wilson's church was called *'The Black Diamond'*, which is an obvious reference to a piece of coal.

How much of Lancashire's pre-Beeching railway lines are still open?

To calculate this would be a mammoth task, but the **Lancashire & Yorkshire Railway Society** tells us that one of their members has calculated that the L&Y Company, which amalgamated with others to become the London Midland & Scottish Railway (LMS) in the 1920s, had 430.43 miles of track in our county, 63.3% of the company's total amount. 65% of those 430 miles are still in use - that's 280 miles. More about the L&Y Railway Society from Stuart Morris, 10 Magna Grove, Sandal, Wakefield WF2 7NG

Why are Bolton folk referred to as 'Trotters'?

It has nothing to do with them walking at a brisk pace or with them having sheep's feet. The word means **'leg-pullers'**. Bolton folk have long been known for their sense of humour. In 1884, *'Timothy Thraddlepin'* wrote a pamphlet, partly in dialect, the full title of which is *'Bolton Trotting, showing how a Relieving Officer took himself to the County Asylum and was detained there whilst his intended patient was enjoying himself at Morecambe'*. In the town's Hall i'th'Wood museum is a painting, dated about 1880. It shows two men, each holding one leg in a bucket of boiling water. They are doing it for a bet. The first chap is in obvious pain, the other is pain-free. This is because he has a wooden leg, a fact which was unknown when the first chap took the bet on. He was the victim of the on-lookers, Boltonians, who are laughing, well, like Bolton Trotters.

Was the first railway ticket a Lancashire invention?

It seems natural that, since the world's first railway passenger train ran in Lancashire, and the world's best-known railway timetable book was devised and published by a Bolton chap called Bradshaw, the train ticket would be a Lancashire invention too. In the early days of railways, Thomas Edmondson of Lancaster, a railway booking clerk, came up with the idea of issuing a ticket using a machine he had invented which gave a number and date on it. His patented tickets became known as *'Edmondson types'*.

Mention of tickets allows me to reach into my family tree album and introduce you to young Jim Bickerton, a clerk snapped in an Oldham, Ashton or Manchester booking office during the First World War. Behind him is a Manchester Evening News calendar.

Are motor cars still made in Lancashire?

Indeed so. The best known factories are at Halewood (Ford) and Blackpool (TVR), not forgetting Leyland's truck and van makers. Blackpool has another motoring association in that the story of Jaguar cars started there in 1922 when the Swallow Sidecar Company, fore-runner of Jaguar, was started. That's why Jag's early model, in the 1930s, was called the SS model. The famous Bond Minicar was made in Preston, just one more example of our industry in motoring.

Was the first fire engine made in Lancashire?

The motorised horseless fire engine is reckoned to have come onto British roads in 1904. However, the Protector Lamp Company of Eccles, a firm still making miners' safety lamps, made one and used it in Eccles in 1901.

Was an eagle ever seen in Southport?

Seagulls - Yes. Eagles - No, unless you are referring to the fact that when, in 1950, the first issue of a boys' comic paper, *The Eagle*, came out, the man behind it and its main characters Dan Dare and P.C.49 was Rev. Marcus Morris, vicar of St. James', Birkdale. *The Eagle* soared until 1970.

Are there any Lancashire townships beginning with the letter 'J'?

Probably not if a township needs to be a place having its own council. Of course, there's Jericho, an area of Bury, and Johnson's Hillock, a small area near the canal at Whittle-le-Woods. In Clarke's *New Lancashire Gazetteer* (1830) is recorded Jackson's Common, a hamlet in the township of Scarisbrick, $2^{1}/_{2}$ miles from Ormskirk.

Did a Lancashire man invent chewing gum?

We can't claim that, but we do know that the world's leading manufacturer, Wrigley's, has a Lancashire background. The main man, P.K. (his initials were also used on his company's products) Wrigley died in 1977 aged 82 years, leaving £58 million to his beneficiaries. His father had started the business after emigrating from the Saddleworth area, near Oldham, where he left many relations. That wonderful writer, Ammon Wrigley (1861-1946) may have been a relative of the Chicago chewer.

Did a Lancashire man invent life insurance policies?

Perhaps that's making too bold a claim, but the insurance companies owe a lot to William Assheton of Middleton (he left there as a lad), who came up with the idea of a scheme for providing annuities for the widows of clergy in the mid-17th century. The scheme failed only through lack of vital statistics.

What part was played by a Lancashire man in the discovery of bottled beer.

Alexander Nowell, Dean of St. Paul's Cathedral was a favourite of Queen Elizabeth the First. From a Whalley family, he was educated at Middleton. He loved fishing, and one day took to the river bank a picnic hamper containing a corked bottle of beer. By chance, he left the full bottle behind when he departed, and on his return a few days later found it to be effervescing. This discovery he passed on to brewers, and today we still benefit from his observation.

Are Victory-Vee lozenges a Lancashire-made product?

Yes - and No. The famous cough lozenge's story started in Nelson in the 1860s when Tommy Fryer, following his grandmother's work, started making 'Cough-No-More' medicated sweets in a small way. He sold out in 1879 to Dr. Edward Smith and his brother William Smith. The Smiths traded under Fryer's name, and moved to larger premises in Nelson in 1890, calling their new premises the Victory Works, a reference to Admiral Lord Nelson's famous flagship. In 1895, by now making Victory Vee lozenges, they registered the Victory trademark, which shows a cannon being fired. Advertising their various lozenges and gums throughout the world brought success. Fryers was bought out in 1965 and ceased production in Nelson. Traditional V-V lozenges are now made by Jackson's of Crediton, Devon. a member of the Trebor Bassett Group.

"SOME MOTHERS DO 'AVE 'EM"

James Robinson Clitheroe was born in 1916 in a cottage which still stands today in the village of Blacko, near Nelson. His love of entertaining people started at a very early age and his dancing and accordion playing soon became a feature of the local village concerts.

Young Jimmy was appearing at the Alhambra Theatre and Imperial Ballroom in Nelson, and having been spotted by *'The Nelson Leader'* newspaper editor, Harold Coulton, was launched on his professional career as one of the touring troupe of *'Winstanley Babes'*.

In 1937 Jimmy, now 21 years of age and standing just 4 feet 2 inches, found himself appearing with Tessie O'Shea on Blackpool's Central Pier, his tap dancing and saxophone playing won him huge applause and within the next few years he began his comedy routine, becoming well-known throughout the north of England. During the Second World War years, Jimmy, now famous for his schoolboy clothes, became the eternal eleven year old and appeared in films with the legendary stars - 'Old Mother Riley', George Formby and Frank Randle.

In the early fifties Jimmy began his now fondly-remembered radio shows, beginning with *'Call Boy'* and followed by *'The Clitheroe Kid'* which ran to over 300 recordings and made Jimmy a huge star. A television series followed in the 1960s. His co-star Danny Ross, playing Alfie Hall, became a perfect partner for Jimmy and made the show a must for the now legions of fans.

When *'The Jimmy Clitheroe Show'* was appearing in Blackpool, the sold-out signs were always needed and he appeared a record **sixteen** seasons. Jimmy became an astonishing sight dressed as *'The Schoolboy'* whilst driving his enormous black Bentley to and from the theatres.

When Jimmy died in 1973 he was mourned by thousands of his fans. In his hey-day his radio shows had audiences of 15 million and his wonderful catch-phrase *"Some mother's do 'ave 'em!"* can still be heard here in Lancashire today.

POULTRY REWARDS

The hen-pen chap was on the down-market side of the leisure pursuits of Lancashire workers. The bands-men, choristers, actors, craftsmen and artists enjoyed a certain cultural cachet. With his cloth cap and muffler, the hen-pen chap found meaning in life by practising the subtleties and intricacies of keeping hens. One such was my father.

He had served an apprenticeship in the running of a pen with his father-in-law. When he finally took the plunge he bought the pen which had been my grandfather's. What he bought, for twelve pounds, was four huts, a selection of troughs, lamps, water-bowls, bins and whatever else was necessary including miles of fencing. The land was rented from a local big-wig. Having launched himself in this career, my father determined to impart to me the knowledge; I became a working partner. For all that it was hard work, it brought me endless pleasures and satisfactions.

Feeding then harvesting

As with any livestock, the well-being of the hens was the first priority. This meant feeding and watering them reliably. During summer evenings, scattering the corn, putting the 'mash' in the troughs and water in the bowls was pure joy. The sound of the hens clucking their approval made sweet music. In the winter evenings things looked different. Dad insisted that in cold weather the hens needed hot mash. This could only be prepared at home, half-a-mile away, so it had to be carried: a hundred hens eat a lot of mash.

We would arrive in pitch darkness, with a bundle of keys bigger than that for Fort Knox. Somehow we would find the *'provin hut'*. There we would light a storm lamp and then lamps for the huts. One of them, a carbide lamp, gave a brilliant white light which so fascinated a hen on one occasion that it crept up beside it, doused the light and then succumbed to the gas. It was quite an adventure, creeping around in the mellow light of a storm lamp, feeding the hens, hearing the occasional squeak of a rat and hoot of an owl and stopping every now and then to warm our hands on the lamp. In the darkness I began to notice the stars.

The flip side was collecting the eggs. During the summer months we would gather 70-80 a day. In spite of my mother baking with them, preserving them in water-glass and serving them boiled, fried, poached and scrambled, and my father swallowing them from the shell like oysters, there was no way we could eat the lot. The result was the development of a modest retail business. We sold them to all and sundry on a weekly basis. One family of six bought them one at a time, for a penny each. This wasn't sufficient to dispose of them during the summer, when the hens, with one or two exceptions, laid as if their lives depended on it, which, these days they would. The surplus we sold to the 'Utility' where we bought the food.

Trading standards

However, it was not as simple as that. The eggs had to be cleaned, weighed and checked for damage and thin shells. This was time-consuming and was rewarded by any weighing less than one ounce and seven eighths bringing a lower price. Those heavier than standard were regarded as being all the same weight, were paid for accordingly. Any damaged or dirty were not paid for at all, but were never-the-less sold on to bakers.

As is the case with unwritten contracts, that between the chap and his hens was subject to disruption by hens which refused to lay. This strike action was known as *'clocking'*, presumably from the clucking sound which they made. This contrasted strongly with the *'Prraaa tuk tuk tuk tuk'* which declared the frantic outpouring of pride and joy in motherhood which accompanied the laying of every egg. A clocking hen seemed mysteriously to double in size by fluffing out its feathers and would sit upon and try to hatch anything vaguely resembling an egg.

Eating but not laying was contrary to the best instincts of a hen-pen chap. A simple procedure was adopted to bring the hen back in line. It was put into a *'clocking box'*, a cage about the size of one now occupied by three battery hens. The perches were so arranged that no more than one foot could be got on a perch at one time. This discomfort, along with short rations, rapidly brought a hen to its senses. Anyone thinking that this was cruel should remember that, today, a failure to deliver would mean immediate transfer to Death Row.

During the winter months the hens concentrated their energies on keeping warm, leaving little for laying eggs. This was seen as an act of God rather than a breach of contract. The hens were fed and we bought eggs to supply our customers, a sort of agricultural sickness benefit.

In the Spring we would buy day-old chicks. Most young things are delightful and none more-so than chickens. They are, however, delicate and had to be placed in a *'brooder'*, an enclosure warmed by a small paraffin flame. The chicks suffered from a fatal tendency to *'go off their legs'* in which condition they would walk on their *'elbows'* to an early grave. To avoid this they were fed cod-liver oil in their meal. Once they developed feathers that danger passed only to be replaced by a greater one, *'pointed neck feathers'*. This was taken to indicate that the chick was more likely to crow than lay and ensured that it was destined to be fried in butter when big enough.

Background skills

In addition to caring for the hens we had to maintain our stock-in-trade. I was taught the arcane skills of straightening nails, making hinges out of leather straps *'borrowed'* from the mill, catches out of wire and fencing out of anything. Huts had to be creosoted outside, cleaned, brushed and whitewashed inside to kill mite. The droppings were bartered for cabbages, rhubarb and black-currants with a neighbouring gardener.

Perhaps the most exciting time was when the *'ratters'* arrived with ferrets and terriers. They made no charge. It was done for the sport, a view not shared by the rats which were quickly dispatched by the dogs once the ferrets had driven them out.

THE FARMING FIELDS OF ECCLES

It is hard to believe that, a century ago, Eccles had a close-knit farming community, with fields running alongside Cow Lane, Catching Lane and wooded Back Lane. The passing years have seen a progressive devouring of this countryside by the housing and industrial estates. Eccles' only remaining claim to agriculture sprawls westward onto Barton Moss.

This faded landscape and way of life can now only exist in fantasy. The changeover did not happen overnight but very gradually, with self-raking reapers replacing scythes and progressing to the horse-drawn binder. Not until the 1950s did the monster of a combine harvester take out the back-breaking job of stooking the sheaves of corn to stand and 'hear' two Sundays church bells before being tossed, sheaf by sheaf, to the loader on the horse-drawn cart.

Dawn till Dusk

A day in the fields began at dawn and, in harvest time, lasted until dusk. Even Sundays were counted as work days and the Church permitted four to be worked during this season to enable the grain to be gathered before the weather broke. Breakfasts and suppers were eaten in the farmhouse; other meals, 'baggins', were sent down the fields in huge baskets. Favourite was crusty, home-made bread with home-churned butter and chunks of cheese washed down with quantities of beer, which was kept cool in thick, stoneware bottles hidden in the hedgerows.

The amounts of beer, often nettle beer, downed was vast. Twenty pints was the standard allowance per man, per day to offset the chronic thirst provoked by the strenuous task in the unshaded sun. It was amazing how they remained sober enough to work!

All God's Gifts Around Us

On the final day of the harvest, the farmer's wife and her helpers spent the day baking and cooking to provide the most important feast of the farming year, the Harvest Home Supper. Wooden bowls of warm 'posset', a concoction of milk, strong ale, sugar and breadcrumbs, were served along with 'Wigg' biscuits for dunking. Sides of beef were roasted, hams boiled and glazed and apple pies baked along with traditional seed cakes and caraway biscuits and

the inevitable pints of ale. The suppers were always a splendid occasion with singing and dancing. They promoted good relationships between farmer and worker.

When beer, food and energy were exhausted, the convivial harvesters fell asleep in the barn on the straw provided, for many were too inebriated to walk home safely along the canal path or along ditch-lined Wood Lane.

"John Ackworth"

Frederick Robert Smith was born at Snaith in Yorkshire on April 18th 1854. His great-grandfather, grandfather, father and seven uncles were all preachers. He was accepted for the Methodist ministry in 1876 and studied for two years, after which he was appointed to his first circuit, Castletown in the Isle of Man. Subsequently he travelled to Worthing, Farnworth, Sheffield, Shotley Bridge, Manchester, Swinton, Lytham, York, St. Helens and Eccles. He came to Burnley from Eccles in 1909, as superintendent of the Wesley circuit. After three years, he retired from active work, but remained in Burnley as a supernumary. An internal ailment afflicted him for several years before his death, on November 13th 1917. He is buried in Burnley cemetery.

He became famous with his first book *'Clogshop Chronicles'* in 1896. From then until 1907 he wrote an almost annual sequence of short stories and novels. He always used the pseudonym 'John Ackworth' for his written work. Ackworth is not far from Snaith.

The man himself

The 'older end' will usually say *"He was a little man, with red hair, and he was a very good preacher."* Those three things stand out. Some will also add that he wrote Clogshop Chronicles. He stood only about five feet high, and could hardly be seen over the top of the pulpit. His hair was very red, though there was not very much of it. He also had a beard - neat, pointed and moderately full.

He had theatrical mannerisms in the pulpit; *"He would shout, and lead up to the shout with a kind of crooning sound"*. Such things can make a man ridiculous, especially if he is physically small to start with, but 'Daddy Smith' held his congregation spellbound. *"To preach was his passion; it was the delight of his life. Knowledge, wit, originality...everything that he had, was used in the work of the pulpit. His preaching consumed him as fire consumes dry timber"*. He was always cheerful. Even when chronically sick, he radiated optimism and friendly humour. He has been described as *'vivacious'*, *'dapper'* and *'rather unorthodox'*. J.R.Bleackley relates how he rather scandalised the stricter Methodists of the Eccles area by riding to his outlying churches on a bicycle. He would sometimes call on an elderly woman and catch her busy with the Monday wash, in which case he would lend a hand with the mangle before departing with a happy *"Cheerio"*.

On one occasion he went with his Sunday School classes on a canal-boat trip. Not only did it rain, but rough children gathered on Patricroft Bridge and dropped sods and small stones onto the boat as it passed under, Mr. Smith's tall hat being a special target. His comment afterwards was characteristically good-humoured: *"A canal-boat trip is a thing that can only properly be appreciated after a preliminary training, and even then requires a peculiar and carefully-cultivated taste"*.

In Burnley, he lived at the Manse on Palatine Square before moving to 122 Manchester Road when he retired. In the last weeks of his life he went to 'Beckside'. a new house on Glen View Road. We can identify 'Beckside' as the present No. 24.

The Smith Family

When he died in 1917, Mr. Smith left a widow, four sons and three daughters. Mrs. Smith (nee Annie Bradley), though not physically small, was so lacking in personality that she is only vaguely remembered in Burnley. She was quiet, kindly, and self-effacing to the point of being rather helpless; *"She would play a part in things but she wouldn't take the lead"*...*"She needed things doing for her"*. After Mr. Smith's death she went to live with her married daughter Margaret (Maggie) at Stockport, who had married in 1907, during her father's ministry at Eccles. Mrs. Smith died in 1943.

Mr. Smith as an author

I regard *Clogshop Chronicles* as a classic of regional literature. It consists of twelve short stories, set in the Lancashire mill-town of *'Beckside'*. The clogger - Jabez Longworth - was the chief official at the chapel and, being of a somewhat assertive disposition, had become the ruling spirit of the village. Long Ben, a tall mild-tempered carpenter, was his lieutenant. Sam Speck, a small-featured man living on a small annuity, acted as henchman to both. Besides these there were Lige the road mender, Jonas Tatlock the choirmaster, Nathan the smith and Jethro the knocker-up. These worthies resort to the clog shop at all convenient times, and there discussed the life of the village. Their conversations and the circumstances connected with them make up the stories.

It is commonly said that everyone has it in him to write one book. *Clogshop Chronicles* bears out the truth of this. If you read its continuation, *Beckside Lights* (1897), you may be slightly disappointed. Mr. Smith never repeated his first success. Although some of his later stories are closely akin to *Clogshop Chronicles*, only *Beckside Lights* comes anywhere near to leaving the reader with the same sense of satisfaction. The rest give the impression of being pot-boilers.

Clogshop Chronicles; the Setting and Characters.

From certain internal allusions - e.g. to the newly-constructed railway line - we can date the setting to about the 1850s and, to me, a great charm of the stories is their evocation of those times long past. The exact identification of 'Beckside' is difficult. R.K.Derbyshire and J.R.Bleakley are convinced that it is Boothstown, but I picture a more Pennine-edge landscape than that. The late Stanley Wood suggested Stoneclough, and I think this is probably correct - or as near correct as any deduction is likely to be, for "Beckside' was probably a composite village. Stoneclough fits well, for we are distinctly told that the clogshop characters spoke the dialect of the Bolton district. It seems to me that Mr.Smith had that part of the Croal Valley pretty firmly in mind. The identification of the characters is a separate issue, and J.R.Bleackley seems almost certainly correct in saying that some of them were based on actual members of the St.Paul's Chapel at Swinton.

His Place in Literature and Drama

F.R.Smith's fiction was within the tradition of regional literature and helped to build that tradition. A contemporary reviewer of *Clogshop Chronicles* made apt comparison with J.M.Barrie's *A Window in Thrums*, and R.K.Derbyshire has categorically said that such homely stories prompted Smith to start writing. More locally, an affinity with the work of Ben Brierley, Edwin Waugh and J. Marshall Mather is obvious. (It is interesting, incidentally, to note that the concept of the clogshop as the unofficial forum of the village men finds expression in the painting by Eastman Johnson, an American, in 1887: *The Nantucket School of Philosophy* shows five old men and a clogger in a setting which could have been taken from Beckside) In a more modern day, Tommy Thompson of Bury continued the tradition with *Under the Barber's Pole*, later popularised by Wilfred Pickles on radio. Stanley Wood (Victoria Wood's father), also of Bury, has up-dated *Clogshop Chronicles* in the form of a successful musical - *Clogs!*

A List of Mr. Smith's books in chronological order

1896	Clogshop Chronicles. Later editions 1905 & 1935.
1897	Beckside Lights.
1898	The Scowcroft Critics and Other Tales.
1899	Doxie Dent: a Clogshop Chronicle.
	The Making of the Million: Tales of the 20th Century Methodist Fund.
1900	The Minder: the story of the courtship, call and conflicts of John Ledger, minder and minister. 2nd edition 1902.
1901	The Coming of the Preachers: a tale of the rise of Methodism.
1902	The Mangle House: a Lancashire tale.
1903	From Crooked Roots.
1904	Old Wenyon's Will, etc.
1907	The Partners, etc.
1909	Life's Working Creed: a series of sermons on the present-day meaning of the Epistle of James.

MED I' LANCASHEER by *Sally James*

Ah wer med i' Lancasheer; it's stamped reet through mi bones,
Un we'er ever Ah do wander, ther's no place quite like home,
Ah've bin to that theer Disney World, un laughed at Mickey Mouse,
Bur Ah allus 'ave a longin' fer mi little Lanky house.
Ah've bin to Greece un Florida, un Norway wi its fjords,
Wer t'German tourists visit un flock theer in ther hords.
Ah've bin to Finland, Sweden, un stepped o'er th'Artic line,
But thers no other sign as friendly as that Red Rose Lanky sign,
Cos ther's coal dust cussin' through mi veins, which pulls mi deawn to t'ground,
Un ther's no other language sweeter thun that broad owd Lanky sound.
Fer Ah've heard um speak i'Germun, i'Norwegian, an' then Greek,
An' Ah've heard 'um speak i'Finnish, but thi ne'er yet heard me speak,
Americuns say sweetly, "Your welcome", and "Have a real nice day",
Bur if Ah spouk in t'Lanky twang, thi'd sey "What's that you say?"
Fer Ah'm like a piece o' Blackpoo' rock, an' stamped reight through mi bone,
Is "This lass is med i' Lancasheer, an' ther's no place quite like home".

(Winner of the Eric Topping Cup for dialect writing,
Fylde Folk Festival, September 1994)

When this photo was taken, around 1905, Thomas Shepherd was licensee of The Bridge Inn, Edenfield Road, Norden. Almost a century on, the pub is still there but the tranquility has gone, as this is now a busy road carrying traffic from Rochdale towards Rawtenstall and the towns of North East Lancashire.

Southport's London Square in the very early years of the twentieth century. The whole place has class: elegant stone buildings, elegant Edwardians walking on the broad streets at a pace matching that of the horse-drawn trams and cabs. The wheelchairs are there to be hired by the aged or infirm. Similar wheelchairs are still in use at Lourdes. What a contrast to the streets of industrial Lancashire towns and cities.

What have Doomington, Yarndale and Thrigsby in common? They are all fictional names for Manchester, which in various novels and stories goes under a variety of disguises. The city is Puddlechester in Catherine Dodd's *Scarlet Gables*, Medlock in Charlotte Fennell's *The Calico Printer*. Cottonborough in William Harrison Ainsworth's *Mervyn Clitheroe* and Drumble in Mrs. Gaskell's *Cranford*, although for her *North and South* she coined another name for Manchester: Milton-Northern.

In 1922 Canon Porteus wrote a poem about the city, *Cottonopolis*. and that title has since been much copied. In Louis Golding's novels set in the Jewish quarter, Manchester goes under the name of Doomington, while in the novels of L.P. Jacks it is Smokeover. Two other novelists, John Carruthers and James L. Hodson, call Manchester Durceston and Burnham respectively, and in 1872 the Rev. Robert Lamb wrote of the place as Yarndale.

Frank Tilsley disguised Manchester as Stockton in *Devil Take the Hindmost (1937)*, and the city became Bleston in Michel Butor's *L'Emploi du Temps* (1957). Thrigsby was the name given Manchester by Gilbert Cannan in his *Old Mole* (1914), and the city has also been identified with the Coketown of Charles Dickens' *Hard Times*, although Preston is another contender for that distinction.

Liverpool may well be the Riversborough of Hesba Stretton's *Cobwebs and Cables*. which mentions the Sefton family. Certainly, this seaport is Gelton in James Hanley's novels concerning the Fury family, just as it is Lowbury in Martin Hare's *Describe a Circle* (1933), Salchester in Winifred Duke's *Household Gods* (1939) and *Counterfeit* (1940) and Lidderpool in the same author's *These are They* (1933). In John Owen's *The Cotton Broker* (1925), Liverpool is Weftport, in Irene Rathbone's *When Days were Years* (1939) it is Hudderspool and in Richard Le Gallienne's *Young Lives* (1898) it is Tyre.

Some disguises are easy to penetrate - no prizes are offered for spotting that Ashlynne in William Quarmby's *Then and Now is* Ashton-under-Lyne. Similarly. Oldingbourne is not a great step from Oldham, putative setting of John Morton Lees's novel *Fine Raiment (c. 1930)*.

Tunstall is hidden in the pages of Charlotte Bronte's *Jane Eyre* as Brocklebridge, and Lancaster features in the writings of Francis Henry Bolton in the *Boys Own Paper* of 1901-18 as Lunechester. Bolton is the Spindleton of Allen Clarke's novels set in that area, and Littleborough becomes Lytelbeorgan in Ben Brierley's dialect story, *Sleawit Bill and the Flood*.

Clitheroe is only thinly disguised as Kempleton in R.T. Bradshaw's *By the Edesion Bridge (1951)*, and Yarrowdale is that part of the county near Walton-le-dale and Chorley described by Brian Almond in his *Gild the Brass Farthing* (1963). Accrington is the town that Thomas Pateman details so well in his *Dunshaw, a Lancashire Background* (1948). Another local writer, Lydia Bland, called it Oakrington.

Almost certainly, Accrington was also Orrington and Carrington in William Westall's novels *The Old Factory* and *Roger Norbreck's Trust*. In those works, and in his *Red Ryvington*. I suspect that Redburn and Whitebrook are Blackburn, and that Moorwell and Waterhead Moor are what we now know as Oswaldtwistle - Westall lived at Stanhill (part of 'Ossy'), which is perhaps the Redscar and Wellsprings of his books.

Turning to the coastal resorts, Greyport is Southport in Hugh Desmond's novel *The Slasher* (1939), and Fleetwood is the Sandyshore of Mrs. Molesworth's *Carrots*. Silverdale is Abermouth in Mrs. Gaskell's *Ruth* (in which Yealand becomes Deepdale), and Blackpool is Northpool in Frank Tilsley's *Pleasure Beach* (1944) - just as that resort is obviously the setting for James Lansdale Hodson's *Carnival at Blackport* (1937), although the author makes a point of saying that 'Blackport' does not exist.

There are, of course, instances in which one can be less certain. Is the St. Aubyn of Julian Prescott's novels in the *Case Proceeding* series really St. Annes? I suspect it is, although there's no conclusive evidence. But then, perhaps you've spotted some clue that I've missed…or maybe you're wondering why I haven't mentioned So-and-So and are itching to add further names to the list …

WELCOME, BONNY BRID

Tha'rt welcome, little bonny brid,
But shouldn't ha' come just when tha did; Times are bad.
We're short o' pobbies for eawr Joe,
But that, o' course, tha didn't know,
Did ta, lad ?

Aw've often yeard mi feyther tell,
'At when aw coom i'th' world misel' 'trade wur slack;
And neaw its hard wark pooin' throo—
But Aw munno fear thee,—iv Aw do
Tha'll go back.

Cheer up! these times 'll awter soon;
Aw'm beawn to beigh another spoon—
One for thee;—
An', as tha's sich a pratty face
Aw'll let thi have eawr Charley's place
On mi knee.

God bless thi, love! Aw'm fain tha'rt come,
Just try and mak' thisel awhoam: Here's thi nest;
Tha'rt loike thi mother to a tee,
But tha's thi feyther's nose, Aw see, Well, aw'm blest !

Come, come, tha needn't look so shy,
Aw am no' blamin' thee, not I;
Settle deawn,
An' tak' this haupney for thisel',
Ther's lots of sugar-sticks to sell deawn i'th' teawn.

Aw know when first Aw coom to th' leet,
Aw're fond o' owt 'at tasted sweet;
Tha'll be th' same.
But come, tha's never towd thi dad
What he's to co thi yet, mi lad, What's thi name ?

Hush! hush! tha mustn't cry this way,
But get this sope o' cinder tay while it's warm;
Mi mother used to give it me,
When Aw wur sich a lad as thee,
In her arm.

Hush-a-babby, hush-a-bee,—
Oh, what a temper!—dear-a-me heaw tha skrikes !
Here's a bit o' sugar, sithee;
Howd thi noise, an' then Aw'll gie thee
Owt tha likes.

We've nobbut getten coarsish fare,
But, eawt o' this tha'll get thi share,
Never fear.
Aw hope tha'll never want a meal,
But allus fill thi bally weel
While tha'rt here.

Thi feyther's noan been wed so lung,
An' yet tha sees he's middlin' thrung
Wi' yo' aw.
Besides thi little brother Ted,
We've one upsteers, asleep i' bed,
Wi' eawr Joe.

But tho' we've childer two or three,
We'll mak' a bit o' reawm for thee,
Bless thee, lad!
Tha'rt th' prattiest brid we have i'th' nest,
So hutch up closer to mi breast; Aw'm thi dad.

David Bowers tells of the boys from Barrow

CHALLENGING THE ZEPPELINS

Lake Constance in Germany and Barrow-in-Furness share the same background in the annals of aeronautical history; these were the proving grounds for the design of naval airships. At the beginning of this century, the Germans had already built the first successful rigid airships which became eponymous with the name of their designer, Count von Zeppelin. Before the First World War, these gigantic zeppelins, buoyed up by hydrogen gas bags and propelled through the air by powerful Maybach engines, were a familiar sight in Germany, carrying passengers and mail. The Germans' immediately latched on to the potential of airships as tools of war. The British were slow to recognise the possible applications. The Admiralty placed an order for the first British airship in 1909. This was to be larger than the German zeppelins.

Designated '*His Majesty's Airship No.1*', work could not commence until a massive hanger had been built in which to construct it. This was built on the edge of the Cavendish Dock and was designed so that an airship could be floated in and out of the hangar on its underslung gondolas - the airship had to be able to take off and land on land and water. The construction of the hangar copied the design used by the Germans. There was one fundamental difference; the Germans built a floating hangar, this could be steered into the prevailing wind so it was easier to manoeuvre airships in and out of the hanger when a wind was blowing across the lake. The hangar on the Cavendish Dock did not have this important feature. At the centre of Cavendish Dock a mast was built for mooring the airship. The docked airship rotated and pivoted up and down if a strong wind was blowing.

Designed and engineered in Barrow

Vickers had limited experience of aeronautical design and they were awarded the contract on the basis of their submarine development work. The Admiralty specification was for an airship which would have a flight duration of twenty-four hours at forty knots. The proposed flight ceiling was 1,500 feet, and the airship was to carry a crew of twenty. Within the hull, which measured 512 feet long and 48 feet in diameter, the gas bags were to have a capacity of 700,000 cubic feet. The framework was to be of a new alloy, duralumin, noted for its strength and lightness. The engines were supplied by a Vickers subsidiary, the Wolseley Tool and Motor Car Company. The Vickers team worked with the Navy under the command of Captain Sueter, with Commander Schwann in overall control. *HMS Hermione* arrived in the dock to serve as their base. In addition to the problems of building an airship with such limited knowledge, Vickers had to contend with the Admiralty's adherence to contract specifications, which were often changed at short notice. Progress was painfully slow and the grumbling craftsmen adopted a derisive name for the airship - '*Mayfly*'. There was a last minute delay when a rating lost his footing and fell through the hull, damaging some of the gas bags.

First appearance

The Mayfly was manoeuvred out of the shed on the 22nd May 1911. It grazed a building although luckily it was undamaged. The workers, sailors, public and notables watched jubilantly as it was towed to the mooring mast where it was left overnight. The *Mayfly* and mooring were put to the severest test when gales of 45 mph sprang up in the night. This gave the designers confidence, although this was dashed when the preliminary trials proved that the *Mayfly* was too heavy to fly. She was towed back to the shed to be stripped of all superfluous equipment. A final rash attempt to reduce weight involved removing the longitudinal framework at the base of

the hull. This was against the advice of one of the principal designers, Hartley Pratt, who prophesied disastrous consequences.

On 22nd September 1911, as the lightened Mayfly was guided out of the hangar his prediction proved to be correct. There was a dreadful rendering as the duralumin girders gave way. The release team panicked as they hauled on the ropes to restrain the bucking hull. Within seconds all that was left of the *Mayfly* was a collapsed envelope of burst gas bags and sodden canvas floating on the dock. A sudden squall which resulted in the handlers losing control and the tail rising suddenly in the air contributed to the disaster, but the weight reduction and removal of the underframe was the real reason for the *Mayfly*'s demise.

A Court of Inquiry was held on *HMS Hermione*. This was attended by Winston Churchill in his capacity as First Sea Lord. Tactfully, Vickers were absolved from blame although there was bitter wrangling over the £70,000 development costs. The challenge to the Zeppelins was abandoned for the immediate future. The *Mayfly* had only managed to fly a few feet off the ground while tethered in the hangar, although the exercise was not a complete loss as the experience gained eventually enabled Vickers to build the first in a line of more successful airship ventures when the successes of the German Zeppelins revitalised interest in rigid airships.

Try again

As the build-up to the First World War gathered pace, the Admiralty placed a new order with Vickers on 10th June 1914. Work started at the Cavendish Dock but was then transferred to a larger hangar on Walney Island. This building was attacked on 29th January 1915 by shell fire from a U-boat commanded by Otto Hersig. His attempt to destroy the firm's airship building facilities were thwarted when he was driven off by the shore battery.

The jinx that haunted the *Mayfly* was finally laid to rest on 27th November 1915 when *Airship No.9* took off and tentatively circled over Walney Island.

SEASIDE SONG PARLOURS

Rummaging among the music in an old piano-stool, I came across an old Lawrence Wright album. Immediately, the pictures started to crowd my mind: seaside delights between the Kaiser War and the Hitler War: arriving in Blackpool on my three-speed bike; going to Yates' in Talbot Road, and there assuaging my thirst and appetite with a sandwich and a mug of tea, which cost a total of fourpence.

I was sixteen, my wage £1 per week, so I wanted cheap entertainment. Then I remembered the Music Shop at North Shore. It was next to Collinsons' Cafe, and was run by The Lawrence Wright Music Company. The idea of these Music Parlours or 'Pitches' was to rent a shop with an open front, install a small stage and a piano, then employ a pianist and a personality demonstrator to sell the sheet music.

In the one near Collinsons, sheet music of a popular song cost sixpence, or you could buy a book of words for a whole series of songs for only fourpence. The artists who demonstrated the songs - mainly Lawrence Wright's - were often well-known personalities. I remember George Mee, the Blackpool footballer, appearing there.

To promote sales, they would ask the stars from Blackpool summer shows to come down and autograph copies of the sheet music. It was essentially a song-plugging exercise. In the early nineteen-twenties, the song publishing companies were already fighting competition from 'the wireless' and from the early gramaphone records.

Being in the charts then was measured in terms of the sheet music sold. There were two great rivals then in Blackpool's Song Parlour field - Lawrence Wright and Bert Feldman. Wright had a split music personality. He published most of his songs under the aegis of his Music Company; but he wrote his songs as 'Horatio Nichols'.

A friend recalls that in the 1928/9 period, whilst she was on school holidays, and her mother was working on the North Pier, she used to elude her mother's notice and slip into the Music Parlour near the Tower. She badgered the manager, Jimmy Calvert, to such an extent, that he let her sing every now and then. She sang songs like *'Have You Ever Been Lonely?'* and *'It's A Sin To Tell A Lie'*. For her daily stint she received the magnificent sum of sixpence. She was delighted!

The greatest hits of those halcyon days, when couples not only sang *'Among My Souvenirs'* and *'Shepherd Of The Hills'* in the Music Shops, but, arm-in-arm with other couples, walked along the promenade singing them.

Who was the first song-plugger? Roberta Dexter, who in those days was known as 'Vivienne Tempest' (great niece of the famous Marie Tempest), claims to have been the first to have been employed by Lawrence Wright. It was in the early twenties - they started at Easter, with Wright playing, and she singing. The songs she remembers from those days include *'Old Fashioned Mother of Mine'* and *'Romany Rose'*. The next year she did a season for Wright in the Isle of Man.

Blackpool had other Song Parlours in the Winter Gardens and on the Pleasure Beach, and other Lancashire resorts were not slow to open similar establishments. Ernest Binns, who ran *'The Arcadian Follies'* at Morecambe for many years, had a pitch only a few yards away from the Arcadian Pavilion. It was only a small one, with a pianist and a singer. There were several other 'pitches' from time to time. Miss Lena Ferrarini, who ran the box office then, recalls that one day the pianist fainted, though miraculously, after a crowd had collected, recovered. If anything, his playing was more spirited than ever. When she congratulated him on his fortitude, she was treated to the broadest of winks!

With the onset of the thirties, the Music Parlours were in decline. Created by Lawrence Wright, the *'Daddy of Tin Pan Alley'*, they had had their glory days. The memory of the man who was one of the pioneers is strong in the minds of the people who met or worked with him.

Wright, a Leicester man, was a workaholic. In 1952 he had a stroke, which paralysed his right hand. Kathleen Eyre, the Blackpool author of 'Seven Golden Miles', recalled meeting him after publication of her book. He gave her one of the last copies of his popular album *'Songs the World Sings'*. He was a sharp man of business, leaving £366,000 when he died in 1964. People still remember his songs and his music. His gift of writing straightforward, popular tunes, was passed on to the people he understood best…the working people of Lancashire!

I'm glad I opened that music-stool!

September 1927, 21 yrs old Charlie Hyland (hatless) and Ken Sharples who worked for Lawrence Wright prepare to distribute copies of 'Me and Jane in a Plane' which is advertised on the side of the van, parked outside one of Wright's song parlours. An aeroplane, containing Wright and Jack Hylton's Band, buzzed over the Promenade, the song being sung from it and copies thrown out as part of the publicity campaign.

THE SUNDAY SCHOOL OUTING

As a child, living in Lancashire, a holiday for me was the annual Sunday School outing. Greece and Spain would be on the agenda one day, but I still remember those trips to the seaside with great affection. We lived in a small village on the outskirts of Manchester. Mum and dad, usually ambivalent towards religious matters actually encouraged my attendance at Sunday school. For peace and quite, they would have sent me to the moon. So, Sunday School it was, and any denomination would suffice. I maximised on this freedom of choice by attending the one which, by reputation, had the best annual day out.

My choice in 1949 was The Evangelical Church of Jesus Christ. They were going to Birkdale, by train. The train journey was the bonus and I signed up, so to speak, for the thirty qualifying attendances that guaranteed inclusion in the excursion party. In comparison, the local Methodist's trip to Belle Vue Zoo seemed very ordinary.

The great day arrived at last and we congregated at the local railway station, seething with suppressed excitement. We cheered loudly when the train appeared, belching clouds of black smoke. Our once pristine shirts and blouses soon exhibited the first sooty smudges of the day. When instructed we clambered into carriages marked 'Excursion'; doors slammed; arms waved excitedly from windows. A blast of the whistle and we were off. The adult in charge of each compartment tried to restore some semblance of order. *"Stop shouting and listen."…"Sit still and keep your feet off the seats."…"Johnny Brown, don't put your head out of the window. You'll get it knocked off!"*

At Birkdale station we formed up like soldiers on parade. The order was given to march off and then teachers dashed about like worried sheep dogs, rounding up the strays. The

Overcrowding? Four classes in one room in an Oldham school in the mid-1930s. These kids may be dreaming of their next Sunday School outing.

salty tang in the air and a distant glimmer of sea lifted our expectations to fever pitch. As we marched we sang hymns. *"Let's sing 'Jesus is my Saviour',"* Mr Morgan, our superintendent, cried in his lilting Welsh voice. Marching ahead of the procession, he would conduct the reedy voices with a flamboyant waving of the arms *"Beautiful, children,"* he would shout. *"Really beautiful."*

Once at the beach, games were played, one following the other in quick succession. Sprints, high-jump, egg-and-spoon; you name it and we played it. By now the white shirts were creased and sweaty, the dresses crumpled and stained. The baptism with blancmange was still to come. At last wooden tables were erected and sufficient varieties of sandwiches laid out to suit all tastes. Meat-paste, tinned salmon, cheese and tomato, sardine; all our favourites were there. Jellies in little paper moulds, trifles, fruit cake, fairy cakes and gallons of orange squash to wash it down. We drooled in anticipation of such a feast. Sea air and exercise, the best appetizer ever invented. Tired and hungry, we waited impatiently to be fed. First though, thanks were offered to our Lord, a rather protracted affair that only prolonged the agonising wait. The word was given at last to form up in orderly lines and the demolition job began in real earnest. Praise be to the Lord and pass the sardine 'sarnies'. Never mind the gritty sand that crunched between our teeth, it was a memorable feast.

Replete, we wandered aimlessly over the dunes and beach. A last paddle in a murky pool. The real sea was still a mile or two away, so the residue from the last high tide had to do. Stones were upturned and bewildered crabs innocently tormented. The sun, a great orange ball, sank slowly below the horizon now. There was an air of sadness as the memorable day drew to a close.

There were no appeals from Mr Morgan to sing hymns on the return journey. It was a subdued and tired collection of children that trekked reluctantly back to the railway station. The Sunday school outing was over for another year. Everyone agreed, it had been the best day ever. My concern now was to select the right school to attend in readiness for next year's trip. Someone told me that the Church of England lot were going to Rhyl. That's for me, I thought. Better get the Christmas party over first though. No point in being too hasty, who knows where the Baptists might be going?

Boring Cases

Recently, the body representing professional engineers announced that it had persuaded the publishers of the Yellow Pages 'phone directory to stop classifying them under the heading 'Boring'. At the same time, a piece of headed notepaper came into my hands. I reproduce it. Readers will see that William Matthews & Company, Artesian Well Engineers, of Moston Lane, Manchester, had a telegraphic code which showed clearly what they did in the civil engineering field. The code, effectively an address, was simply 'Boring, Manchester'.

In the same envelope was this 1913 letter from S. Noton & Sons of Oldham - Telegraphic Code 'Fibre, Oldham'. They were invoicing the Manchester City Combing Company for a special stout fibre box, 42 ins by 24 ins, 36 ins deep, with 1 inch tongue and groove pine bottom - a really sturdy thing with two handles on each of the long sides. It cost £2.5s.

Both companies were represented at the Manchester Royal Exchange each Tuesday and Friday, and both were in the ABC 5th Edition, which I presume was a trade directory.

Another interesting point is that Noton's charged 5% on overdue accounts.

Two examples of the delightfully pictorial stationery of those days - not boring at all.

38

A First World War Letter

A letter from Cpl. T. Whittaker of Burnley to his friend and fellow soldier Herbert Dutton of Atherton, a Quartermaster/Corporal in the King's Own Royal Lancaster Regiment

Monday, May 29th, 1916

Dear Old Pal,

I now take the Pleasure in writing you a few lines as I know how you will want to know my experiences in the boxing ring. Them were the days Dutton. Well, I have been in hospital with swollen feet but it was with standing in the trenches up to the knees in water. You know 8 days is a fair while to be stood up and we never got to close our eyes all the time. You might not believe it but it is true enough and the Germans sent their gas over and 78 were gassed and when the artillery start, they don't send shells, they send foundries over.

What a life Dutton. I could not make you believe what it is like. There was some mines blown up and believe me, I thought it was lights out and the ground trembled like a jelly. We were only 25 yards from the German trenches, so you will understand why we had no sleep. I had a private in my sentry group. It got on his nerves to such an extent that he went stone mad. Directly after, a shell came and hit a fellow from Nelson but he was in fragments and I picked up his top lip with his tash on. So you will have an idea of what it is like here.

Harper is here and he is no friend of the men. They do not like him. Swallow is here and Wright. As regards my first coming out here we landed at a place and stayed there about a week and we were sent up the line to another place on the 2nd April which was a Saturday and on the Sunday, we joined the battalion and at about 4-30 the O.C. came and said we had a trench and crater to take and at 6-30 we set off to our task.

When we had gone so far, we had to get our faces blackened and off we went again. At 2-10 on the Monday morning, we had got to where we had to make the bayonet charge and before I knew where I was, I had fallen in a German trench and of course, I was a bit dazed but I soon jumped up when I heard someone shout "*Mercy Comrade*". It was dark and I had a job to find out where the noise was coming from, so I felt with my hand on the floor and I could just feel the head of the German. He was buried all but his head - wait for it - and then seven came walking towards me with their hands up asking for mercy but they got it. I can assure you Dutton it is no picnic going into a bayonet charge. It is not like charging sacks. Then after the charge comes the bombardment. That is worse than the charge.

Remember me to Bob Jones 42 and Sgt. Major and the Q.M., I mean Hulton. Is French with you yet?

I will draw this letter to a close with best wishes for your welfare. I will tell you what Dutton, I could do with some tackle to clean my buttons as we have to clean them when out of the trenches. So no more this time from your old pal Whit. Buck up. Write back soon Dutton as I shall not be here long. Address as follows.

Cpl. T. Whittaker 16731 K.O.R.L. Regt.
No.1 Convalescent Camp, Boulougne

THE KING'S OWN

CLEGG HALL MYTHS AND LEGENDS

There cannot be a more atmospheric setting for one of Lancashire's most famous 'boggart' tales than Clegg Hall, near Milnrow. Looming above the soon-to-be-restored Rochdale Canal, the hall, dark and gloomy looking, is the archetypal haunted house. In its semi-ruined state it probably appears even more sinister than when it was inhabited. The windows, long since devoid of glass, peer out across a landscape much changed since Bernulf de Clegg built the first Clegg Hall on this ancient spot. In time the timber-framed hall which he built was replaced by the much sturdier stone-built hall we see today. Despite long neglect, the outer walls still stand strong and firm; inside though, not a vestige remains of the fine panelled rooms and vast stone fireplaces. Perhaps it was around these log-burning fires that the legend of the Clegg Hall Boggart was born. In those dark and distant days, winter evenings would be spent around the roaring fire listening to tales of ghost and boggart. The wind howling across the stark Lancashire landscape would add to the stories; an authenticity unmatched by today's television sets.

The timber-framed hall is where the story of *The Clegg Hall Boggart* originated. Sometime during the thirteenth or fourteenth century, it is said that a tragedy akin to the 'Babes in the Wood' story occurred. An evil-hearted uncle plotted to destroy the two orphaned heirs to the Clegg estate. One dark and stormy night he ensured they slept well by giving them a sleeping draught. Having made certain that no one remained awake to witness his treachery, he took the children from their cots and, without a moment's remorse, threw them into the dark waters of the moat. Still drugged, they could not cry out and so they died a cruel death to satisfy their uncle's greed. Thus the legend began, though it was not the spirits of the children which forever after haunted the hall, but that of the uncle, whose soul could not gain peace.

The hall has had a mixed fortune during its almost four-hundred-year history. It became too large for one family to occupy and from the beginning of the nineteenth century it was reduced to the status of a public house known as the *'Hare and Hounds'*. At a later date the name was altered to the *'Black Sloven'*. A tenant farmer ran the public house and resided in part of the hall. The back part was divided into several tenements. Refreshments were served in the old kitchen - quite an experience!

In 1869, by which time the name had been changed back to the *'Hare and Hounds'*, the licence was withdrawn. The long road to the ghostly ruin we see today began. Perhaps the final indignity was being used as a very *'stately'* hen house. One wonders whether the presence of the boggart had an effect on egg production?

Clegg Hall is also noted for its very sophisticated exterior details, mainly the projecting two-storeyed porch with baluster columns. It was one of the first buildings in the district to be built on the 'double pile' principle. Even in its ruinous state it remains a very 'powerful' building. There could be no worthier setting for this ghostly tale.

The preservation of the hall and the surrounding industrial hamlet caused a storm of protest several years ago. A private concern wished to purchase the hall and its environs, in order to make it the centre-piece of a kind of Lancashire equivalent of *'Disney World'*. This did not prove too popular with local residents though, and the plans came to nothing. The hall is now in the care of **'Pennine Heritage Trust'**. With the impending restoration of the Rochdale Canal, perhaps something can be done to preserve Clegg Hall and resident boggart for future generations, before it crumbles away and becomes part of Lancashire's lost heritage.

✻ ❀ ✻

THE NEWLY-REGISTERED VENTILATING HAT.

THE attention of gentlemen is respectfully directed to the following circular of Mr. W. Mayhew, hat maker, London:—

" Registered 1st March, 1844.

" An important improvement in the manufacture of the velvet hat, combining all the qualities of thorough ventilation,—much desired by gentlemen wearing the velvet hat,—of which many complaints have been made of their *noise* and *vibration*, and *heat* to the *head*, so creative of serious maladies.

" The material composing this *beneficial* object has a negative quality, being a non-conductor of heat, and unaffected by any change of weather or climate, keeping the head in a cool state of temperature.

" The important advantages of these hats are, that the perspiration is allowed to escape; and thus they are always kept dry inside, and free from that greasy appearance round the band, near the brim, which other hats, after being worn a short time, invariably show; and which is principally caused by the return, in a condensed state, of the vapour of the head.

" Many gentlemen of the medical profession having worn them, have expressed a decided approval of their ventilating qualities.

" The great desideratum, a ventilation in hats, requires no further explanation; and the improvement now introduced will effect it in a far higher degree than can be stated in an advertisement. Manufactory, Union-street, Southwark.

" W. MAYHEW, Registrator."

Sold only by W. MOUNTCASTLE, Hatter to the Queen, 21, Market-street, Manchester.

A True Tale by Norman Holme

JUGGLIN' WI' FAWSE TEETH

When thar't gerrin' on a bit thi mind seems fer't dwell mooer in't past, and wi aet ony reyson at aw summat as tha's ne'er thowt abaet fer yars pops into thi yed. Like t'other neet when Ah wur sittin' in t'cheer awum, smookin' a tab an' bein' mindful o' nowt in particler, Ah fun misel thinkin' abaet a mon cawed Dicky an t'lowf as he gin us o'er some fawse teeth.

Mony a yar agoo, when Ah warked in th'hospital administration i' Bowton, thur wur a chap cawed Dick, a nursin' orderly fro' Owfen. (Westhoughton, fer them as caun't speyk gradely) We aw cawed 'im "Scrawp Yed", or "Kaew Yed" bur 'e ne'er took no heed. Sithee, if tha'd skenned abaet fer a month o' Sundays tha couldn't a' met a mooer cheerfu' mon, notwithstondin' as aew 'e'd getten flattest feet in't Northern Union. Ah allus thowt if thi'd 'ad a championship fer flat feet 'e'd a bin th'onds daewn winner, if tha understonds mi meynin'. Gooin' up main corridor tha meight 'appen on 'im three of four times in a day, an' every time wi' aet fail 'e'd ax thi:

"Ar't awreet?" *"Nobbut middlin' tha knows, Dicky."* *"Aye. Same road wi me an aw."*

Then 'e'd gi' thi a grin like a Cheshire cat an' shuffle off, 'is feet slurrin' abaet like weet kippers on a smack shop caenter.

Nethen, one day they geet short o' nurses on th'owd ladies' ward ('Jerry hat ricks' as they wu cawed) an' thur wur nobbut Dicky available. I' them days a mon couldn't wark on t'female wards, but seein' as it wur an emergency, an' what's mooer aw patients wur seventy or eighty yar owd, it wur thowt as it meyt not matter o'er much if Dicky lent a 'ond. When 'e geet theer, 'e could see as t'ward sister wur flummoxed regardin' wark as 'er could gi' 'im.

"Ah'll tell thi what, Richard," 'er said, usin' 'is Sunday name, *"Thur's forty patients an' thi'n aw geet fawse teeth. Sithee, it'll 'elp if tha con gi' um a gradely cleyn."*

Dicky did nowt but grin afore startin' at fust bed an' axin patient fer 'er fawse teeth. Well, 'e geet agate scrubbin' an' polishin' until them teeth favvered like brond new. It war var near dinner time afore 'e'd finished cleynin' aw on um, an' that's when 'e fun aet as thur wur a snag. When Ah say aw on um, a meyn aw on um at same time. Dust see, 'e'd collected forty sets o' fawse teeth i' one bowl, so 'e wur faced wi' eighty dental plates wi' aet knowin' which belonged wheere. Tha con just imagine t'performance as thur wur in matchin' top an' bottom sets on t'reet patients. It took a wik afore they'd getten' it sorted aet and bi then everybody 'ad yed warch, an' 'appen rung teeth an aw! Ah wur towd as when t'relatives visited at neet tha could yar 'um sayin: *"Eee, Gronny, th'as put weight o' thi face sin we seed thi last wik."* *"Oh aye, well it mun bi these new fawse teeth thi'n gi' mi."* *"Ah ne'er thowt as thi'd gi' thi new teeth at thy age. Well tha lives un' larns."*

Sometimes an owd lass u'd cowf like a good 'un, an' 'er top set ud goo whizzin' aet an' land on t'flooer. Others shrieked a bit when it wur fun aet as they'd getten wrung teeth i' thur maeth.

"Dust know, thi'n takken mi teeth an' gi me these, an' thur nowheere near as good as them Ah 'ad in afore."

In th'end we aw 'ad a lowf abaet it, but Dickie wur ne'er axed fer t'cleyn ony mooer fawse teeth. Ah thowt it a bit 'ard on 'im, seein' as aew 'e wur a reyt gradely warker, an' ne'er minded thi cawin' 'im "Scrawp Yed".

MORNYCASH, The Lancashire Lad

The dicovery of a sheet of music for a song called *"If tha' comes from Lancasheer"* (the cover is reproduced here) prompted me to find out something about Morny Cash, pipe-smoking, trilby-wearing singer.

Fame

Morny Cash appears to have been his correct name. He was born in Manchester in 1872, and became an engineer. With a friend he made appearances as comedy duetists, and when appearing at a charity concert, they were spotted and booked by a variety agent who gave them their first professional engagement. It was in Blackpool and they received five shillings each.

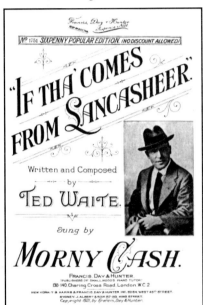

Turning solo, Morny became well-known in the Manchester music halls. He certainly worked in the famous Leeds City Varieties Music Hall and in New Brighton. The turning point in his career came when he appeared at the Roscommon Music Hall in Liverpool. In the early years of the century, he topped the bill in a Blackpool theatre, probably the Empire, and became popular in the South where he toured as '**The Lancashire Lad**'.

Essentially a dialect comedian, Morny specialised in portraying old men and singing comic songs, some of them full of double entendre, with titles such as *'All of a do'*, *'Beautiful, beautiful bed'*, *'Married a year today'* and *'I live in Trafalgar Square'*.

> Hurray, Hurray, I'm going to be married today.
> For years I've been up on the shelf
> But now I'm going to slip myself.
> Hurray, Hurray. I've often heard folks say
> The older the fiddle, the sweeter the tune.
> Fancy me at 63 having a honeymoon.

Formby

Similar in style to George Formby Senior, Morny made records. Whereas Formby's gormless character always ended up losing, Morny's simpleton always won. Typical of this is his recorded song *'My Ninepence'*, in which, given an unwanted rail ticket to London, he draws all his money (ninepence) out of the bank and sets off. He visits the West End, walks into all sorts of traps for the innocent, but gets home unscathed, still with his ninepence in his pocket...

This most popular of Northern dialect comedians died in October 1938.

A LAW UNTO HIMSELF

In the good old days of not so long ago, say forty or fifty years back, when all policemen seemed to be six feet plus, with chins like Desperate Dan and fists like legs of mutton, many barbers supplemented their income by repairing umbrellas, and in many shops a tea chest of damaged 'brollies' in the corner was as much a part of the furniture and fittings as were the barber's chair and razor strop.

At this time, (the post war years) the ranks of Wigan Borough Police Force were graced by the presence of an officer who we shall call P.C. Fred Ashton, because that wasn't his name.

P.C.Ashton was an excellent officer in many respects. He knew the borough like the back of his hand, he knew its 'villains' even better. He did however have two weaknesses, if weaknesses they may be called; he was an inveterate practical joker, and he had an exceptionally keen and witty tongue that he couldn't keep in check. No *'esprit de l'escalier'* for P.C. Ashton; if he thought of a lightning riposte or particularly juicy *'bon mot'*, he came out with it, and to hell with the consequences.

It was said by P.C. Ashton's colleagues, that he had worn a path across the Chief Constables's office carpet, on his regular visits to answer to complaints made by both his supervisory officers and humourless members of the public.

On these visits, two things generally served in P.C. Ashton's favour; firstly his many years police service, and secondly the fact that the Chief Constable was possessed of a robust sense of humour himself. As a result of these factors, he usually received a king-sized rollicking, and escaped the fines and other unpleasant disciplinary measures the Chief had at his disposal.

One particularly filthy, wet, Monday morning found our hero in helmet and cape, standing outside Wigan's North Western Railway Station, cursing the weather, and the fact that he had a *'point'* to keep in less than ten minutes, which precluded him from seeking shelter anywhere. (A point was a pre-arranged time and place where his sergeant knew he would be)

As he made to move in the direction of his point, a squeaky, irritable voice at his elbow made P.C. Ashton aware of the fact that someone was trying to gain his attention. Turning around, he found himself standing chest-to-nose with a short, stout, red-faced gentleman, immaculately dressed in bowler hat, wing collar and 'city' suit. The following dialogue took place:

P.C. Ashton (PCA) *"Nah then what con Ah do for thee owd lad?"*

Bowler-hatted Gent (BHG): *"Firstly you can cease calling me 'old lad' and adopt a more civil form of address."*

PCA (evidently chastened) *"Very sorry Sir. Can I help you at all."*

BHG (feathers still ruffled) *"I have just got off the London train, and in alighting, have torn the fabric of my umbrella in the carriage door lock. Is there a barber's shop or similar establishment locally, that could carry out the necessary repairs whilst I conduct my business in town?"*

PCA (respectfully) *"Certainly Sir. If you go under the railway bridge, take the first left, which is Queen Street, you'll find Livesey's premises a short way down on the right hand side."*

BHG (still ruffled) *"Oh really. Is that a barber's shop? Do they repair umbrellas?"*

PCA (bending down, nose to nose with BHG) *"Nay owd lad, it's a builder's merchants, but 'appen they'll put a **** slate on it for thee!"*

(Exit P.C. Ashton leaving BHG speechless).

Postscript

It transpired later that the bowler-hatted gentleman was a barrister, whose business in the town that day was to prosecute for the police at Wigan Crown Court. As can be imagined, he did not delay in bringing the matter to the attention of the Chief Constable, who in turn, brought it to the attention of P.C. Ashton in a rather forceful and financially disadvantageous manner. But as P.C. Ashton later remarked; *"It were worth every penny just fer't see yon mon's face."*

PREVALENCE OF SCARLET FEVER : A WARNING.

The Medical Officer of Health for Salford requests us to publish the following :—

The Medical Officer of Health wishes to draw special attention to the prevalence of a most severe type of scarlet fever in several districts lying just outside the boundaries of Salford, in the hope of putting the inhabitants of the borough on their guard against a possible epidemic visitation of the disease at home.

He would direct attention to the necessity for personal and general cleanliness, especially in the removal of refuse matter of all kinds from the neighbourhood of dwellings. He would caution people against the common but most dangerous practice of needlessly visiting infected houses whilst disease is still present, or before such houses have been disinfected and cleaned ; and he would strongly recommend the immediate removal of infected persons to the Wilton Hospital in Cross Lane. The Medical Officer of Health will, on receiving information of the occurrence of infectious disease, immediately send a skilled inspector to disinfect premises, to remove exist-ing nuisances, and generally to give assistance and ad-vice to persons requiring it ; and he hopes that the public will show a little more readiness than they have hitherto done in availing themselves of this offer, which has so frequently been repeated, by giving such information as will enable him to do this. There are a disinfecting stove and a feather washing apparatus at the hospital, and the authorities will be glad to disinfect any bedding or other articles which cannot be conveniently washed, conveying the same to and from the hospital in a van specially provided for the purpose.

The Medical Officer of Health feels it to be his duty to reiterate a warning which he has previously uttered on more than one occasion, in the hope that Salford may escape the severe epidemic which is now raging within so short a distance of her borders.

Mike Clarke, a historian of the Leeds & Liverpool Canal, writes on

THOMAS STEERS

Thomas Steers, involved in the planning and construction of river navigations and canals since 1712, who built Liverpool's first docks and was intimately connected with the development of the town for forty years, is almost unknown. Probably born in Kent in 1672, he may have been present at the Battle of the Boyne in 1690. He appears in the Army List of 7th July 1702 as a Quarter Master in the Fourth Regiment of Foot (The King's Own). The regiment served in the Low Countries so it was probably here that Steers learnt about canal and dock building. Steers returned to Kent in 1697, two years later marrying Henrietta Maria Barber. They lived in Rotherhithe, where the Howland Great Dock was under construction, and he may have been employed as surveyor to the Howland Estate.

Liverpool's First Dock

How then did Steers become involved in the construction of Liverpool's first dock? One had been suggested in 1708, and Sir Thomas Johnson wrote to Richard Norris that he had spoken to George Sorocold about its construction. (Sorocold, perhaps the country's leading engineer at that time, was born in Lancashire.) He drew up a plans which were used to obtain an Act of Parliament in 1710. However, Sorocold did not want to become engineer for the project, and Steers was chosen instead. On 17th May 1710 the Town Council were informed that he had arrived in Liverpool. Why was Steers chosen? A possible explanation is that whilst in the army he had come to the notice of the Earl of Derby, who was in Flanders commanding the 16th Regiment of Foot.

Steers was responsible not only for the dock's design, but was the contractor for the excavation work. It was open for shipping by mid 1715, but improvements continued to be made until 1721. The work cost considerably more than envisaged by Sorocold, and to raise capital, a second Act was obtained in 1717. This also authorised a dry (tidal) dock and three graving docks. Further expansion was suggested in 1718 when Steers drew up plans for a southward extension. By 1721, with the new Customs House finished, Steers reported to the Council that the Dock was complete.

The Douglas and the Mersey & Irwell Navigations

In 1712 Steers proposed improvements for navigation on the rivers Mersey and Irwell to Manchester, and the Douglas to Wigan. Although neither proposal received Assent from Parliament at this time, they were both successful in 1720. Steers was named in both as one of the undertakers.

The Douglas was the first to receive Royal Assent, just in time for the South Sea Bubble and the subsequent financial scandal. The other undertaker, Squire, who went to London to raise money, seems to have been carried away by the temptations of the time and sent north little of the money invested in the navigation. Steers, in Lancashire, had started at Rufford, building locks and straightening the river, but little work was undertaken because of finance. The navigation was not completed until 1741, after it had been taken over by Alexander Leigh of Wigan in the 1730s, who sometimes called in Steers to advise.

Work on the Mersey and Irwell was authorised later in 1720, and missed the financial problems of the Douglas, though it took almost as long to complete. It is probable that Steers was the navigation's engineer. Henry Berry, who was to take over as Dock Engineer on Steers' death, and who subsequently built the Sankey Navigation, also helped Steers when he was working on the Douglas.

Steers was involved with commerce. He was a promoter of the unsuccessful Liverpool Waterworks, and was one owner of the vessel *DOVE*, trading to the West Indies. He had other shipping interests. In 1746 he was part owner of the sloop *HOADLEY* which traded with Ireland. He also owned an anchor smithy near the Dock and built five houses in Derby Square.

He was involved in local politics, became a Freeman in 1713 and was elected to the Town Council in 1717, becoming one of the Bailiffs in 1719 and 1723, and Mayor in 1739. He was an Out-Burgess for Wigan by 1746, possibly through his connection with the Douglas Navigation.

Steers was a member of the controlling group on the Council and an employee. In 1717, he was appointed Dock Master at an annual salary of £50. William Braddock was Water Bailiff, but in 1724 Steers took over this post, his salary was stopped and he had to rely upon the fees and perks associated with the posts. The finances of Town and Dock were inextricably linked. By 1725 income from the Dock was sufficient to finance the construction of the Corporation's church, St.George's. Steers drew up plans and estimates with James Shaw. Built on the site of the castle, it took seven years to complete. Steers was responsible for the foundations and steeple.

In 1725 he was appointed a commissioner for the turnpike to Prescot, while in 1737 he advised the Council about the Weaver Navigation. He was also responsible for the seaward approaches to the river, checking the buoyed channel on Hoylake Bank in 1736. The next year he presented plans for a new dock and pier, needed to reduce overcrowding.

In 1727 Steers became a patron of the arts when he leased the playhouse in Chorley Street, subsequently opening a new theatre on the site of the Old Ropery in 1740. A concern for the less well off can be found during his period as Mayor in 1739 when he erected, on waste land belonging to the Corporation, several houses for poor seamen.

From 1729, for twenty years, Steers worked in Northern Ireland on the Newry Canal, River Boyne and Ballycastle harbour. He did much innovative work and kept up his relationship with Henry Berry, who used Steers' ideas later when he built the Sankey Canal.

Later Work in Lancashire and Yorkshire

Steers continued to improve the dock in Liverpool. In 1738 an Act for a new dock was obtained, with Steers overseeing the work. It was still incomplete in 1750 when he died, and opened in 1753, finished by Henry Berry.

Despite his age, Steers undertook a wide variety of work during the 1740s, such as a survey for the Calder and Hebble Navigation, assisted by John Eyes. John Smeaton used it when he built the navigation later. Architectural work in Liverpool included a survey of the Exchange building, in 1740, design work on the new Exchange, in 1748 and advise on the stone for St.Thomas' Church. During the '45 rebellion, he had been responsible for fortifying the town.

He died in 1750, aged 78, and was buried in St.Peter's Churchyard. His death was only mentioned briefly in the Town Records *"Whereas Mr.Alderman Steers is lately dead, it is ordered that Henry Berry, late clerk to him, be continued to oversee the works till further order."* The only other contemporary account of his work is in a letter from John Smeaton to the Calder & Hebble Committee in 1757, saying that he was using Steers and Eyes survey of the rivers. He could rely on this as *"...those gentlemen were generally esteemed men of character and ability in their profession, particularly Mr.Steers..."* It is fitting that the sole commendation of Steers work should come from Smeaton, the father of the civil engineering profession.

These clog-shod lads are bemused by a photographer as they stand, about 1912, at the corner of Killon Street and New Alfred Street, Bury, which is a splendid example of terraced housebuilding in brick with (quality) stone embellishments and cast iron garden railings. The block was designed to contain its own corner shop, with flagstones replacing the garden area. The gas lamp has had its glass fittings removed or broken (by these scallywags playing football or throwing stones?)

A superb photo taken in the early 1920s in Bolton's Deansgate; paviours laying cobbles, which were properly called setts; public transport; gas lamps; wooden barrows and carts; all men wearing headgear. It's a warm, sunny day because the men have taken their jackets off and a shop has its sunblind down.

Photographs bearing a date on them are a boon to local historians. Here we see men at work on the public transport system in Smallbridge in May 1905. Clearly it wasn't taken on a school holiday. Look at the photo - not a brick in sight.

This photo, taken on May 3rd 1854, and must surely be one of Lancashire's earliest dated photos. Chatburn church steeple has been repaired since the photo was taken, undoubtedly by the men who turned up with a horse and cart. Did the steeple have a lightning conductor? I bet one was fitted when the repair work was done.

GRANDMA

Grandma was well-known and highly esteemed. She had been widowed at the age of 36 and had brought up her family of five in addition to managing the confectionery business which she and her husband had founded. Eventually, her two sons and three daughters married and she was blessed with eight grandchildren, seven boys and myself. Being amongst my male cousins meant that my childhood was spent playing with train sets, model cars, toy garages and farms, forts and soldiers, and in outdoor pursuits such as 'Cowboys and Indians', fishing, sledging and cricket.

Cricket

Grandma was a keen cricket fan, probably due to the fact that she lived opposite Colne's cricket field. She had a splendid view of the pitch and scoreboard from her upstairs windows and every summer Saturday afternoon she was to be found watching from her vantage point.

Invariably, her grandchildren would join her to see the match, as we soon realised that this was a much more economical and comfortable way to see the cricket rather than paying to go inside the ground. There were two large windows in her bedroom and we arranged chairs in appropriate situations to take full advantage of the unrestricted view. At times it could be hazardous as it was not uncommon for damage to be done to windows when batsmen sent the ball hurtling over the high wall, across the road. There was one occasion when a ball smashed through Grandma's window, striking and breaking the back of a bedroom chair. The tea interval was always welcome and Grandma would appear with beaming countenance and a trolley laden with sandwiches, home-made cakes and her highly-acclaimed trifles.

Manual Dexterity and Methodism

She was a splendid cook and baker, and an accomplished needlewoman and worked many beautiful tapestries and embroidered tablecloths which she presented to her children and which still exist as family possessions. Being the only girl, she tried to pass on her skills to me; with little success. Needlework in my hands was something of a disaster. I know that she was very pleased to have a girl in the family, but I fear I never came up to her expectations regarding feminine pursuits and domestic skills.

She was closely connected with our Methodist Chapel where her husband had been a local preacher, and all her family were brought up as Methodists. The chapel benefited from her many generous monetary donations and gifts of a pulpit cover and a communion rail. She suffered from rheumatism which, in later years, prevented her from attending chapel, during which time our minister often visited her in her own home and he always stayed for afternoon tea. In fact his visits were so frequent that I was highly suspicious that it was his addiction to Grandma's trifles that were the main attraction, rather than his concern for her spiritual needs.

Grandma's birthdays were always celebrated in style as family and friends congregated bearing gifts. The table was set with a hand-embroidered table cloth, fine china and silver tea-pot. A tempting meal including home-made cakes and trifle was enjoyed by all.

When Grandma went out, her progress was slow, majestic and stately as a galleon. She wore a fox fur and a hat trimmed with feathery plumes. I recall one occasion when Grandma came to our house for tea and during the meal my budgie escaped from his cage, headed straight for the table and promptly fell into a full jug of milk. I rescued him from drowning and he ascended to alight on her plumed hat, which she was wearing at the time. Milk mingled and merged with the feathery fronds forming rivulets which dripped from the brim. To us, this was hilarious, though Grandma was not amused. Being afflicted with rheumatism, she relied heavily on a walking stick which came in very useful for poking and pointing at objects when she was being curious or critical. In her later years her sight deteriorated to an extent where she could no longer see sufficiently to execute her fine embroidery, so then she appreciated my company for a game of cards. Being Methodists we did not play for money.

On leaving school, I became employed at my father's garage which was situated within sight of Grandma's house, so that when she was progressing slowly towards our premises wearing her fox fur and plumed hat, I had just sufficient time to dust the office, tidy the papers on my desk and hide a few things behind cushions before she arrived with her ever-critical gaze.

Her home was a large family house with an attic and basement, and in earlier years the basement had been the living accommodation for her newly-married eldest daughter and her husband. When they moved on, the basement became my mother's sewing room for her dressmaking business, and its final role was to accommodate the youngest daughter's knitting machine, which led to the foundation of a well-known firm of knitwear manufacturers.

An Empty Nest

When the family were all married and living in homes of their own, she decided to employ a maid who slept in the attic and lived in the kitchen. The maid was a very lively and likeable person and soon made friends with the whole family. When she married and left her employment, Grandma replaced her with an older person who was a companion housekeeper, and she became part of the family.

Grandma died at the age of 90, and at her memorial service, whilst the trifle-loving minister eulogised about Grandma's many fine qualities, my pearl necklace broke. Despite clutching myself in a frantic and fruitless effort to contain the pearls, they descended noisily on to the wooden floor, clattering like hail on a tin roof and shattering the peaceful atmosphere.

We all missed Grandma very much, as she and her home were the hub and meeting place for the entire family. Though many years have passed and strangers occupy her house, I still have vivid recollections of her birthday celebrations, her delicious trifles, her plumed hats, the cricket matches and the beautiful tapestries and embroideries which have become our treasured heirlooms.

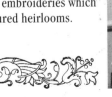

An advert written by Joshua Lysons of Pendlebury in the 1880s.

J. C. BARKER,
Clog and Patten Maker, Newsagent,
AND GENERAL DEALER,
Near CHRIST CHURCH, PENDLEBURY,

Is prepared to supply the Public with the following Articles:-

Periodicals and Bristles,
Cobblers' Wax and Penny Whistles;
Pattens, Clogs and Daily Papers,
Startling Tales for midnight tapers;
Almanacs of various names,
Books of pleasing fireside games;
Monthly Magazines, Pomatum,
Nuts - too many sorts to state 'em;
Valentines in great variety -
Suitable for all society;
Tales - religious, social, moral,
Neckbeads very much like coral;
Tales of past and present times,
Sparrowbills and Nursery Rhymes;
Tales of goblins, imps and spectres,
Air Balloons, and Mursell's Lectures;
Strings for big and little Fiddles,
Mormon Works and Books of Riddles;

Books for Sunday, Scholars' Prizes,
Tobacco, Pipes all shapes and sizes;
Bibles, Sealing Wax and Figs,
Readying Combs and One-inch Sprigs;
Brickdust, Prayer Books, Scented Soap,
Toothache Pills and Bands of Hope;
Sugar Toffy, Books of Martyrs,
Spurgeon's Sermons, Ladies' Garters;
Eccles Cakes, and genuine too,
Bury Simnels, Powder Blue;
Paper, Rubbing Stones and Sand,
Copy Books - in every hand;
Magnesia, Blacking, Weekly News,
Any Book you like to choose;
Teaspoons, Tablespoons, and Spices,
Fine Cigars of various prices;
Tobacco, British Workman, Snuff,
Knives, and Mustard - sharp enough;

Toys for Children, Helps for Nurses,
Oranges, and Fancy Purses;
Wesley's Portrait, Albert's, Bunyan's,
Cloggers' Chips, and Pickling Onions;
Congreve Matches, Fusees too,
Ladies' Twist for those who chew;
Pens of Steel, and Pens of Quills,
Purgative and Stomach Pills;
Clog-clasps, Apples, Ink, Bootlaces,
Holders for Cigars and Cases;
Rings, and India-rubber Teats,
Revival Hymns, and Humbug Sweets;
Hair Oil, Clog Nails, Pencils, Slates,
Perfumery. Pigtail, Plug and Dates;
Sweets - in all their preparations,
Jack-i'-th'-Box, and Gough's Orations;
All these, and more than I can mention,
Invite the Public's kind attention.

AN OLD CHRISTMAS TRADITION

It was an old tradition at Christmas time
In the County of Lancashire,
For folk to sit on stone benches
Cracking nuts round a circular fire;
They were the sons and daughters of weavers,
And folks all makes of trade;
And with this gradely Lancashire tradition
Many a good match was made.

There was hand-bell ringing, and Christmas choirs,
House to house in gay accord;
There was songs of cheer and Christmas psalms,
And the carols of Wynkin de Worde;
All the churches were decked with evergreens
Like the Druids did long ago;
So the spirits could hide in the branches
From storms and winter snow.

There were boys performing old pantomimes
With blackened faces and brooms;
And riding hobby horses through crowded streets
Dressed in silk ribbons and plumes;
"Here I come with my broom!' they would cry,
"Nobbut little David doubt;
And if you will not give me some brass,
I will sweep your houses out!"

Another old tradition were 'penny on the hob'
For the first to let Christmas in;
There was boggart tales and childrens games,
With prizes of toffee to win;
There was Simnel Cakes, mince pies and goose,
Black puddings on Christmas morn;
With braggot ale, turkey, and Poulton beef,
And food for the poor and forlorn.

We still drink and dance the old year out,
And remember dead kith and kin;
And neighbours still call with a cob of coal
To let the New Year in;
We still kiss the lasses under mistletoe,
And as of old, in Lancashire,
We still practise our Christmas traditions
With pride, goodwill, and cheer.

LORD MAYOR OF MIDDLETON

Thirty years ago or so our pleasures at Easter-time were simple ones. A trip to a seaside resort not too far away seemed the height of luxury, but today many people set their sights on an air trip to Paris or the South of France for an Easter holiday, or at least a weekend at one of our own resorts. In my own memory we always seemed to be making for the fields and hills on foot. There is still the annual pilgrimage of city dwellers into the hills of Derbyshire, to the lanes of Cheshire, and some make the long trek up the Pennine Way.

I remember that there were always the bunched-up groups of cycling clubs, with the fast and slow groups, straining to do the allotted miles each day whatever the cost. Today these have mostly been pushed off the roads by cars. Simple as our pleasures seemed, we have to go further back still to find that even they made a sharp contrast with the almost primitive amusements of our forefathers at the public holiday times. Life was hard then, both on the land, in the workshop, and in the home… No electricity, no washing machines, no fridges or modern cookers, no TV or radio, little public transport.

It takes little imagination to conjure up the life of any woman in the 1800s. Housework from the first light of day, with cooking, mending and sick-nursing thrown in. Looking into the records of those times we find that life was lived with a pretty powerful punch, and some of our so-called holiday hours, frustrated by crowds and traffic jams, seem pale and tedious by comparison.

'Black Knight'

For them the long dark winter had to be struggled through with stoic endurance, the weakest going to the grave. Only *"Symnel"* Sunday, when the rigorous diet was relaxed for one day, brightened the long days of Lent.

Easter brought light and life, and by the time Good Friday was over everyone was in the mood for revelry, to eat, drink and be merry. Each district had its own way of

This pair are Chadderton Fold's first two 'Mayors', Charlie Graham (left) and David Schofield. The tradition was devised by Sam Broadbent of the Church Inn in 1935. Taking office, Charlie said to great applause, that he would have a bath in public. By this he intended that he would try to get public baths built. He was treated to a free quart of ale each Sunday. Chadderton Fold still has a 'Mayor'.

photo: Geoff Graham

enjoyment, from rolling pace-eggs, morris dancing and holding processions. In these processions there was always a central figure to either admire or to deride.

The ceremony of "*Riding the Black Knight*" was performed on Easter Monday at Ashton-under-Lyne, when an effigy clad in armour, was mounted on a horse and paraded through the streets. At an appointed place the figure was placed in a shooting butt, and everyone who had a gun fired bullets till they were tired. There is little doubt about the origin of the "*Black Lad*" when history records the ways of Middleton's first Sir Ralph Assheton, known to this day as the Black Knight.

Easter Day was spent in prayer and praise in the parish church, then, on Easter Monday, everyone donned new clothes to walk proudly down the lanes to visit friends and relations. In the weeks before Easter the girls had spent their spare time making elaborate new gowns and hats, putting hours of sewing into bead and braid trimmings. Styles and colours were kept a secret from their friends, so on the appointed day there was a grand fashion show.

Mock Ceremony

The men had new shirts and footwear, and a man with a new pair of "feightin'" clogs sallied forth, looking for the first fight with the light of battle in his eyes. The men resorted to the ale houses where they drank and fought with a will. It was the done thing to have as many fights as possible, and at the Old Boar's Head a room was set apart, known as the "Thrashing Room", where men wrestled and fought each other for hours at a time.

On the Tuesday evening as the light was fading, the most intoxicated fellow among them was elected the new "*Lord Mayor of Middleton*" with mock ceremony. His coat was torn off his back and replaced by a dirty, old jacket. His face and hands were daubed with soot and a pigtail tied to his head. He was then tied to a chair - if "*too far gone*" - and was duly proclaimed "*Lord Mayor*". By this time the clock would be sounding midnight, and then they all sallied forth to conduct him through the streets to call on his "loyal" subjects.

Sleepless Night

There was no sleep for anyone in Middleton that night, for the procession paraded through the town till the morning, shouting for the "Mayor's" dues at every house. With the coming of dawn many of his followers dropped down where they stood to get some sleep, before the revelry started again the next day . Sometimes damage had been done to property, and it was the job of the police to find out who had broken this or that window, but it was a hard task when all the town was involved.

Rude and unsophisticated these amusements seem to us, but we have to remember that the whole background of living was very different from today. Surrounded by hardships their pleasures were also hard and rough, and it was no disgrace to get "*as drunk as a lord*" when the beer was cheap and the ale houses many. The custom lingered on to the turn of the century, and a few old men can still remember the making of the "*Lord Mayor*". The last time the procession was held it began at Plunder Town, Throstle Nest, which is now at the top of Mellalieu Street. (There was formerly a large house in the woods called Throstle Hall). Nothing could keep the Middleton men from the Mayor-making, and one old inhabitant can still remember her father rushing off to join in, when she was a little girl. In those days the men drank and fought, but now the men drink and drive, and who shall decide which is the greater evil?

by Jan Hawthorne

WHERE HAVE ALL THE BOGGARTS GONE?

In modern times things that go bump in the night are more than likely to be nocturnal intruders of the nasty and mortal kind rather than ghostly supernatural agents returned from the grave to plague the living. In olden days this was not the case. Every square mile of the Lancashire landscape was troubled by twilight visitors of another breed. **Boggarts!**

Barns, bridges, farms and halls played host to these spirit creatures and folk would complain of the mischief they carried out. Descriptions of what boggarts looked like or what exactly they are differ considerably. Jessica Lofthouse said the Boggart was a shy half-man half-spirit creature who when he did put in an appearance tended to be *"no more than knee high, his face wizened, his neck scrawny like an old man's, his arms thin, his legs looking incapable of supporting his corpulent body."*

At other times he would appear as a large dog with great arms *"whisking tail, hair black as soot and his rollin' een (eyes) big as saucers"*!

His purpose in the land of mortals is debatable. In Well Hall Cottage, Clitheroe, he was the welcome visitor to one old lady for whom he swept, polished and spring cleaned. Wolfen Hall, Chipping, was overrun by a boggart of the most terrible kind who kept the owners awake at night with shrieks and howls. Some times he would grow so angry that he even threw things about. This boisterous boggart was banished by use of bell, book and candle.

A similar fate awaited the boggart that tormented the citizens of Longridge in the 1650s. Rafe Radcliffe called in the priest to lay to rest this boggart underneath a slab of rock which can still be seen today on the approach to Written Stone Farm, Ribchester. The boggart's grave bears the inscription *"Rauffe Radcliffe laid this stone to lye forever A.D. 1655"* and is said to keep the evil spirit at bay. Woe-be-tide anyone who moves it!

Are They Out There?

So abundant once, what has happened to all the boggarts now? Are they still with us? Where are they hiding?

The most famous boggart of all must surely be that which tormented George Chetham and his family at Clough Farm, North-east of Manchester prior to 1830, at a place that is now called Boggart Hole Clough. The family were at their wits end by the evil doings of their unwanted guest and decided to *"do a flittin"* to escape. Unfortunately as they climbed aboard their possession-filled cart to make good their flight a neighbour stopped them and asked what business they were about. Before George could answer up pops the boggart and says *"neighbour were flitting!"*

This story was first reported by Wigan folklorist John Roby in his *Traditions of Lancashire* (1829) but like so many legends it had its origin far removed from where we now associate it. The story was

56

given to Roby by T. Crofton Croker who had told the same story in his Fairy Legends (1825) about the doings of an Irish Cluricaune, one of a trio of Irish solitary fairies (the others being the far darrig and the leprechaun) often described as *"an old withered little man"* Although a lovely story, there is little doubt that the tale has no basis in fact.

This demonstrates one of the problems of hunting for boggarts. It seems the term 'boggart' was often used to describe what in other locales are called 'goblins', 'fairy folk' and 'trolls', with their tales being adapted to fit into the local folklore. This is nowhere better demonstrated in the writings of the Atherton folklorist, Arthur Griffiths, who, in his book *Lancashire Folklore* (1993) collected together some boggart tales. He refers to humans as 'forkypeds' and the boggarts as being evil sprites of the bog lands under the control of the devil himself, 'Owd Hob'. One is left in no doubt that the boggarts (and 'Ullerts' and 'Besoms') referred to are creatures made up to fit a story-telling need.

Bell, Book and Candle

It would be wrong to dismiss all boggart stories as merely imaginative. Some do have a basis in fact.

The Boggart of Written Stone Farm and the Wolfen Hall Boggart both appear to have existed and both were successfully laid to rest using bell, book and candle, an early form of exorcism used to remove evil spirits from either a possessed person or place. The ceremony derives from a much older church service of excommunication where a sinner would be barred from worshipping by a priest who would toll a small bell, slam shut the bible and then extinguish the holy candles to show the miscreant he was no longer welcome.

Still Active

On the Beech Hill Estate, Wigan, in 1982, the Simpson family of Guilford Crescent complained of a presence in the house that not only billowed the curtains, turned the television on and off but also tried to drag them out of bed. At Ashurst Hall Farm, Dalton, in 1980, Paul Tyrer was attacked by an invisible creature that dragged him out of bed and threw him to the ground. As he fled his bedroom *"I could hear what ever it was rustling and shuffling behind me."* Next door to the White Lion Pub on Church Street, Upholland, once stood a house that in August 1904 became the centre of much attention when curtains flew unaided from the windows, bricks pulled themselves from walls and books whizzed around the room. Had the Simpson's, Mr Tyrer and the occupants of the Upholland house been blessed with a boggart coming to stay? They did not think so. They put their disturbances down to ghosts. This is where the next difficulty comes when tracking down boggarts. Much boggart activity is now regarded as the work of the modern poltergeist - a noisy, destructive spirit which plagues homes and businesses.

In answer to *"where have all the boggarts gone?"* I would have to say I do not know. The modern idea to class boggarts as a catch-all for Lancashire ghosts (similar to the way Cumbrians use the word 'boggles') is wrong. The boggart should have a place in any Lancashire folkloreist's heart to rival the leprechaun.

John Cochrane tells of
SOUTHPORT'S FIRST CAR

In 1996, the motor industry celebrated its centenary and many famous names were remembered. What is often forgotten, is that, all over Britain amateur engineers were poring over any information that they could find concerning these new machines. Everywhere there were repairers of bicycles and sewing machines, builders of boats and steam engineers, and many others, sitting, thinking, drawing and working. Most did not get beyond the thinking stage, although they may have ended up as vehicle repairers rather than innovators.

One of these enthusiasts who actually produced a working motor car was Felix William Isherwood Hudlass, of Southport. He was born in Manchester, in 1874. His father and uncle were Singer sewing machine repairers. They diversified into any other light engineering activity that would use their acquired skills and make a profit. They also had a vague involvement with a firm called the Nestrop Gas Engine Company.

Tinkering Instead of Doctoring

Felix was a delicate child, and so, on the death of his mother, in 1886, the family moved to Southport. They settled in Hartwood Road, and transferred the sewing machine business there. Felix had to abandon his ambition to become a doctor, and entered the family firm, but not to repair sewing machines. He had shown a great interest in photography, and was an accomplished pianist. He became an agent for the Nestrop Company's '*Pneu*' camera, and, as well as repairing and servicing other photographic equipment, designed his own camera. The 1895 Southport directory listed Felix Hudlass as a photographic dealer and music teacher.

His real interest however was centered on a group of sheds in Ivy Street. Here, in his spare time, he became one of that exclusive band who brought the motor car to Britain's streets.

Unbelievable

Felix started to build his first car towards the end of 1895 and by the following summer it was completed and running. Incredibly, all the parts, including sparking plugs and carburettor, were hand made in the Hudlass workshop, now grandly called the Pheonix Motor Works. Amazingly, young Felix, up to that point, had never seen another car. The first car that he ever saw was his own creation!

This vehicle was of about 5 h.p., and featured open leather-belt transmission, which provided two forward speeds, but no reverse. It had a claimed top speed of 15 m.p.h., well in excess of the current 2 m.p.h. urban limit! This first car was fitted with hand made iron tyres, but these proved to be dangerously slippy on the granite setts of Southport's roads. As an alternative, rubber tyres from a horse-bus were used. Their $1\frac{1}{4}$ inch width made them less slippery, but they exactly matched the groove of the tramlines, with, occasionally, interesting results!

Hudlass sold his first car to a local doctor, Sargen Tordoff of Ash Street, and this was the first car to be seen on the streets of Southport. His other early customers included a Doctor Barrett, who eventually bought the Pheonix Works, and John Nowell, joint maker of the very successful '*Gardwell*' bicycle.

Although a new model was announced every year between 1897 and 1902 it is doubtful whether more than twenty cars were sold in all. This gave Hudlass cause for financial concern.

He wrote a letter to a long standing friend in Southport, in the 1940s. An extract shows how difficult it was for any aspiring entrepreneur to gain financial help from the stalwarts of the staple industries on which British capital was based.

"…when I was making cars in Southport, and was running short of cash, I approached a wealthy cotton spinner (who had shown interest in me), *if he would finance me* (he could have found £5,000 as easily as I could find five shillings)*"*. This is roughly what he said. *"Hudlass, I think I can claim to be a successful businessman and I have had a greater experience than you, and I would willingly find all the money you want if I could see any prospects of a return. But I can see no future for the motor car and I would advise you not to put any more money and time into this business…"*

Hudlass left Southport in 1902 having sold the Ivy Street works to Doctor Barrett, who continued to market the cars under the name 'Phoenix', and later, 'Barcar', but eventually abandoned the business. The original sheds are still there, now used as a builder's yard. Hudlass obtained a post as a mechanic in London. In 1903 he was appointed to the position of Chief Engineer at what became the Royal Automobile Club in 1907. He stayed for 44 years until his retirement, in 1947, at the age of 74. He was succeeded by his son Maurice. During the First World War, Felix was seconded to the army vehicle depot at Boulogne. There he was in charge of vehicle servicing and for his work he was awarded an O.B.E.

He kept up with many contacts in Southport, and on his retirement, he constructed a scale model of his first car, which he presented to the Botanic Gardens Museum in Churchtown. He died in 1966 at the age of 92.

Felix Hudlass at the controls of his first motor car in 1896. Watch out Southport!

A WHITSUN TRAGEDY

Whit Monday fell on June 10th in 1878. On Morecambe Bay the weather was fine but with a strong wind from the south-west. Fleetwood, growing as a seaside resort as well as a port, was expecting large numbers of day-trippers to arrive by train from central and east Lancashire, and all was set for a busy day. However, when the first of the visitors began to emerge from Fleetwood Station around mid-morning they found no festive atmosphere. Shops and businesses were closed and the streets strangely quiet. Fleetwood was in mourning. Why?

Across the River Wyre, no more than a couple of miles from Fleetwood Station, a tragedy had taken place a few hours earlier. A boat carrying a happy family party had sunk with the loss of six lives; the shock had made itself felt in Fleetwood as well as in Knott End, where the victims had lived. Three of the dead were Bagots, a well known fishing family whose members lived in cottages on the bank of the river, directly across the estuary from the station at Fleetwood. The other three were lifelong friends of the Bagots. The family had fished the Bay for generations and knew its waters and its moods with an intimacy born of long experience. Why?

The reason for the party being at sea that morning was the annual Whit Monday Sports Meeting at Lancaster, one of the main attractions being the wrestling tournament, 'Cumberland and Westmorland' style, in which Richard Bagot, brother to three of those in the boat, was to take part. Richard was a wrestler of considerable standing who was reckoned to stand a very good chance of winning this prestigious event, and his family and friends were travelling from Knott End to cheer him on. For them it was a holiday occasion and it was a happy group of young people that set out at half past four that morning.

There were seven in the boat. Owner of the two masted sailing vessel, *Nymph*, and in charge that day was John Bagot, aged 33, who had spent all his life working in Morecambe Bay. Next came Hezekiah, his brother aged 28, another experienced Bay fisherman. Harriet Bagot, aged 24, sister to John and Hezekiah was present, together with her fiancee, John Woods aged 31, yet another who had spent his life in the waters of the Bay. The fourth member of the family present was Thomas Hardman Bagot, aged 6, son of the boat's owner, and enormously enthusiastic both for the journey to Lancaster and for his uncle's victory in the wrestling. The other two were close friends of the family: Henry Porter, aged 24, a farmer's son from Knott End, and John Cowell, an apprentice ship's carpenter from Fleetwood. Someone who should have been there did not turn up. The missing member of the party was Leonard Billington, a farmer's son from Pilling Lane, who had a little further to come than any of the others. When four thirty came, and Leonard had not arrived, the others agreed that they could not wait for him as they still had to cross to Fleetwood for Cowell before setting out for Lancaster.

A journey from Knott End to Lancaster in 1878 was very difficult. The road through Pilling, Cockerham and Thurnham was little more than a rutted track in places and in any case, the tide would be covering much of it where it runs across the marshes of Pilling and Cockerham. The Bagots were well aware of the tide time that day and knew that if they attempted to go by road a long detour would be necessary. The route they must follow was obvious.

They would go by boat and follow the deep-water channel of the Wyre out into the bay until they came to the equivalent channel of the River Lune, up which they would proceed until they reached Sunderland Point. There they would leave the boat and take a pony and trap the remaining few miles.

Having picked up young Cowell, they were on their way down channel by four forty five, sailing at a spanking pace. John Bagot was in no doubt as to the proper course to follow. He must keep to the deep water, first in the Wyre and then in the Lune. Morecambe Bay is very shallow along most of its shoreline, and between the Wyre and the Lune at low tide the sea recedes a long way, exposing miles of seemingly flat sand across which the channels of both rivers meander until they reach deep water far out. Had it been low tide when John Bagot took his boat to sea that day he would have had no option but to stick to the deep water. The tide, however, was high and those in the boat could see to starboard the whole of Preesall Sands and Pilling Sands covered to a considerable depth. To cross the sands instead of following the river channels seemed a very tempting short cut and some suggested taking it. There were, however, at least three men in the boat who knew just how dangerous this could be. There was a high tide and a strong wind which made the sea rough. In the deeper water of the channels and further out in the bay this was not a problem as the waves there, large though they might be, do not break. It is only when the tide has covered the shore and the water is shallow that the waves are made to break by beating against the seabed.

Debate followed the initial suggestion that they cross the sands; John Bagot allowed himself to be persuaded that this was acceptable. He put over his helm and turned the boat to starboard, leaving the Wyre Channel and heading for Sunderland Point by the direct route, which would have been denied him if the tide had been other than high.

Spirits in the boat were excellent and they were making a very good speed. The men settled back and lit their pipes, with the wind, now almost directly astern, filling the sails and driving them swiftly towards their destination.

Leonard Billington arrived at the moorings to find that the party had left without him. He was late and he knew that time was precious, so, although disappointed, he understood why they had had to do it. He set off for home along the sea wall at around five o'clock and when he reached his father's farm at Pilling Lane he stopped and looked out to sea. A mile or so from where he stood he saw a boat that he recognised and realised that John was taking the short cut. The sea was rough and there was a lot of white water but the boat was clearly making good progress. He was joined on the sea wall by his father and for some time the two of them stood watching. Then they lost sight of the boat, assuming she had been hidden by spray.

What the Billingtons had seen was not the temporary obscuring of the boat. There arose on the port side of the 'Nymph' the biggest sea that John Bagot had ever seen, and before anything could be done or said, it turned its crest and broke directly above them. Tons of water descended onto the boat, forcing it to the bottom. All but two of the party, happy and relaxed a few seconds earlier, were swept away in an instant and drowned. The water, however, was of no great depth and Nymph's keel was firmly resting on the bottom leaving the upper part of her masts protruding. John Bagot, without any knowledge of how he came to be there, found himself holding an oar in one hand and clinging to a mast with the other. His sister, Harriet, was holding on to him with her arms around his neck. Brother and sister clung to their precarious hold as wave after battering wave tried to dislodge them. A brief conversation took place, Harriet saying she could hold on no longer and John assuring her that he would not let her go. Harriet was torn away from him by the waves, and she was lost.

John Bagot, a man at the peak of his strength, was able to maintain his hold on both the mast and the oar, and was able to make a decision. He would release his hold on the mast and, using the oar as a float, would attempt to swim towards the shore until he could find the bottom with his feet. He let go and struck out for safety. It is not clear as to how long he was in the water but before six o'clock the Billingtons saw a man carrying an oar staggering through the shallows towards them. Recognising John Bagot they dashed to his assistance. They took him to their nearby farmhouse where they wrapped him in blankets and gave him brandy. Horrified, they listened to what he had to tell. Not long after six, the postman called and he spread the story quickly around the district. By six thirty there were horses and carts on the beach to pick up the bodies, and within another hour, everyone in Fleetwood seemed to know also.

The Coroner's Court

On Wednesday July 12th, an inquest was conducted at the Bourne Arms Hotel, Knott End, by the Coroner, Mr. Holden. The only witness with any relevant testimony was the survivor, John Bagot, the owner and skipper of the boat and the most experienced in the party. A verdict of 'Accidental Death' was returned and condolences offered to the bereaved families. A matter of particular anguish to John and his wife was the fact that the body of six year old Thomas was not washed up. It was never found.

Four identical gravestones stand side by side in Preesall cemetery, bearing testimony to the events of that day. Henry Porter, John Woods, Harriet and Hezekiah Bagot are buried as they had lived and as they had died - together. Thomas Hardman Bagot's name appears on Harriet's gravestone but his small remains lie somewhere in Morecambe Bay. John Cowell is buried at Fleetwood.

Doubly Tragic

Hezekiah's wife was expecting a child which was born a few days later; Harriet Bagot and John Woods, due to be married within weeks, were never to stand together at the altar; little Thomas, whose parents could never give him a proper burial; John Cowell was the seventh son his parents had lost in tragic circumstances. John Bagot, the man who could have prevented the tragedy had he not allowed himself to be persuaded to take the short cut, lived for another twenty four years. No one blamed him but there can be no doubt that he blamed himself. His death, on September 25th, 1903, came no doubt as a release from the torment of his memories. His gravestone, identical to those of his companions, stands a few yards from theirs.

Finally, we consider Richard Bagot, without whom the happy party would not have been making its way to Lancaster. Like his brother John, he too must have carried a great burden. Evidently the dreadful news had reached Lancaster before the wrestling tournament began, for Richard Bagot, favourite to win, took no part in it.

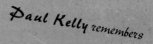
Paul Kelly remembers

THE SORCERER.
(DEDICATED TO TOM FINNEY)

A fleeting shadow, flying down the wing,
dummying defenders, who can't do a thing.
An ephemeral figure, floating like mist,
leaving opponents shaking a fist.

A feint of the foot, a twist of the hips,
an eager crowd, licking its lips.
A dazzling skill, set to disarm,
all those in range of his magnetic charm.

An expectant buzz fills the ground,
one more opponent left to round.
A hopeful tackle, but he's too quick.
As deft as a conjurer, doing a trick.

An arrow-like shot spreadeagles the net.
As perfect a goal as you're likely to get.
A split second silence freezes the scene.
An act of perfection, so graceful, so clean.

The opposing fans join in the cheers,
totally oblivious of their team's arrears.
Not a single thought, or hint of derision.
Just an entranced mass, saluting a vision.

63

BEER LACED WITH ARSENIC

The case of Holt v Wren (1903), involved a builder's labourer from Blackburn with fixed, if not particularly temperate, habits. He drank four to six pints daily and always at the defendant's public house, which was tied to Holden's Brewery. He fell ill with arsenic poisoning from the beer and successfully sued the publican, getting £50 damages.

The incident was part of an epidemic of arsenical poisoning from contaminated beer in 1900 and early 1901. At least 6,000 cases had been identified nationally but the true figure was probably higher due to the disease not being recognised. A considerable number of deaths also occurred but many were associated, wrongly, to other causes such as *"alcoholic neuritis"*. The pattern of sickness was very patchy with about 2000 cases in Manchester, 1000 in Salford, 650 in Staffordshire, at least 100 and probably 1000 in Liverpool and 950 in the administrative county of Lancashire. Many areas had no cases and wide variations occurred between adjacent places. For example Blackburn had 15 cases, Accrington 14, Darwen 34, Padiham 12, Haslingden 2 and no cases at all were reported from Oswaldtwistle, Rishton, Clayton, Great Harwood and Rawtenstall.

In general the south, east and west of England together with Wales, Scotland and the areas bordering Scotland were unaffected. The cause of the poisoning was found to lie in the glucose and invert sugar supplied to a number of breweries by the Liverpool company Bostock's. Only those using Bostock's glucose and invert sugar experienced the problem. Individual drinking habits determined which individuals suffered illness. One man for example had been teetotal for 6 months then drank 42 pints in two days and went down with acute arsenical poisoning!! He recovered after a couple of weeks in hospital. There was a lot of heavy beer drinking with over a third of a Salford sample of 150 drinkers consuming well over four pints per day and a numbers drinking 12 pints daily. Always obtaining beer from the same establishment increased the risk of poisoning which, in part, explained why the epidemic seemed to effect women more than men. Women tended to either drink at a single public house or at home, obtaining their beer from a single convenient source. In some areas they got a *"double pull"* or *"long pull"* in their jug paying for one pint but being given one and a half.

The arsenic content of the beer was high with Holden's brewery beer analysing at between 0.12 and 0. 57 grains of arsenious oxide per gallon and Whewell's of Blackburn containing even more. A level of 0.05 of a grain per week was considered a dangerous level of intake over an unlimited period, as arsenic tends to build up in the body. The intake of arsenious oxide for moderate drinkers in affected areas was estimated at one grain per week with those drinking over four pints per day getting a weekly dose of two to four grains. The worst beer sample analysed during the epidemic contained one and a half grains per gallon. Bostock's glucose contained up to 0.13% by weight of arsenious oxide. This could account for over two grains of arsenic per gallon of beer. Most beers were brewed with a mix of sugars from more than one source however.

The arsenic got into the sugar due to a change in the type of sulphuric acid used by the sugar company in its manufacture. The acid came from one source, Nicholson and Sons of Leeds and contained between 1.5 and 2.5% of arsenious oxide. It was in fact a saturated arsenic solution. It was a murky area of dispute between Bostock's and Nicholson's as to how the cheaper arsenic containing acid came to replace the more expensive arsenic free product previously supplied. Nicholson's sent seven to ten tons of acid to Bostock's weekly for eight months which meant about four to six tons of white arsenic in all went into their sugars!

The epidemic even affected children, with two cases of infants being poisoned through their mother's milk, and nine-week old whose mother had been taking stout to build herself up for five weeks previously. A two year old girl in Bacup, the daughter of a publican, got "*sups*" of beer from customers and went down with poisoning, as did an eleven year old girl whose father worked in a brewery. She had made toffee from arsenical glucose.

Public concern was matched by the brewers, who, with almost no exceptions, responded very quickly once the problem was recognised, promptly withdrawing and destroying hundreds of thousands of gallons of beer - £1,800 worth in Holden's case. The government responded rapidly, setting up a Royal Commission in February 1901 (the problem having been recognised first in November 1900) which produced its first report in July 1901.

The final 1903 report contained sound proposals to prevent any recurrence of the problem, recognising the validity of the Salford Medical Officer of Health's view that anyone replacing a substance used in foodstuff manufacture by another must take responsibility for "*seeing that no injury shall ever result from such substitution*". The Managing Director of Newcastle Brewery summed up the industries attitude, observing "*any recommendation that will safeguard the public would protect the brewer as well*".

One cannot help reflecting, in the light of the BSE problem, that we used to do things better! Certainly we have had no beer problems since and both confidence and the safety of the product were restored within weeks of the problem being identified.

LIVERPOOL GAS-LIGHT COMPANY.

SCALE OF CHARGES PER ANNUM,
For Burners of Various Sizes,
Calculated for Lighting to the Hours below mentioned.

One Argand,	Till 8 o'Clock,	Till 9 o'Clock,	Till 10 o'Clock,	Till 11 o'Clock,	Till 12 o'Clock,
	£. s. d.	£. s. d.	£. s. d.	£. s. d.	£. s. d.
No. 1,	3 0 0	3 18 0	4 16 0	5 12 0	6 8 0
No. 2,	2 14 0	3 5 0	4 0 0	4 14 0	5 8 0
No. 3.	2 2 0	2 14 0	3 7 0	3 18 0	4 10 0
One Batwing,	2 14 ·0	3 5 0	4 0 0	4 14 0	5 8 0

One Batwing, all night, £7. 7s.

Persons who wish to take the Light, may make application at the Company's Office, No. 62, Dale-street, corner of Hatton-garden.

Innkeepers and others, whose Hours of Lighting are irregular, may be accommodated by making a special agreement.

No extra charge will be made, if the light be extinguished in a quarter of an hour after the time contracted for, and on Saturday Evenings the Company will allow burning till Twelve o'Clock.

The Rents will be collected at the commencement of each quarter, (after the first,) and will be divided as follows : two thirds of the above prices for the two winter quarters, and one third for the two summer quarters, and handsome discounts will be allowed to those who take three or more burners, viz. for three burners, £2½ per cent. ; for four, five, or six, £5 per cent. ; for seven, eight, or nine, £7½ per cent. ; and for ten or more, £10 per cent.

The Branch Pipes will be brought just within the Houses at the expence of the Company, and Mr. Varty is appointed by the Committee, and recommended to the Public to fit up the Lamps, Burners, &c. in the interior. His terms may be known at the Office, where patterns and drawings of Lamps, &c. may be seen.

Committee Room, Sept. 6, 1816.

Les Bond takes us below stairs at the house of Sir Loin of Beef

HOGHTON TOWER:
THE MAINTENANCE OF A TRADITION

Midway between Preston and Blackburn, just off the A675 Preston Old Road and overlooking the Lancashire Plain, stands Hoghton Tower, one of Lancashire's well loved landmarks. Stand at the roadside entrance and the famous drive (was it really carpeted ?) rises majestically. The outside world almost ceases to exist as the ascent into history begins.

The great castellated house is planted squarely on the crest of the last southwesterly hill of the Pendle Range and from it on clear days, several hundred square miles of Lancashire and beyond may be seen. Erected in the second half of the 16th Century by Thomas Hoghton, the house has remained with the De Hoghtons and is currently home to Sir Bernard De Hoghton, 14th Baronet, and his family. Their line may be traced directly, on the male side, to Walter, a companion of William the Conqueror and on the female side to Lady Godiva of Coventry, Wife of Leofric Earl of Mercia.

The Magnificent Seven

The estate looms large in the history of the County of Lancashire. Today threequarters of the house is open to the public and plans are in hand to give public access to even more areas of it. What is probably not realised by many is the immense amount of work which goes on to enable Hoghton Tower to function as it does The De Hoghtons and their staff work tirelessly to ensure that such a unique treasure survives the modern day pressures for which such buildings were not designed: the magnificent condition of the house is a credit to them all.

Maintenance of the Estate is entrusted to seven members of staff. Eileen Flannagan and Christine Daniels take care of the administration. Both began working in a part-time capacity and now have to work full-time to ensure smooth running. Organising functions, such as the annual fireworks display to the music of the Liverpool Philharmonic, can take hours of paperwork and phone calls. The result is a truly wonderous affair.

The polishing and dusting and general cleaning is carried out by Jo Davies and Maggie Throup. Yes, when they have finished you certainly can see your face in it. Ian Barrett, Estate Foreman, and his son Nick, along with Brian Wiggins, look to the building renovation needs of the estate. Says Ian, *"Renovation and maintenance of such buildings require special skills forgotten by modern craftsmen."* He continues, *"An awful lot of research has to be carried out before many simple tasks can be attempted. It would be very easy to cause severe damage to the buildings using modern materials and techniques."* Ian cites the barn as one example. A timber roof truss had rotted causing a partial collapse of the roof. The roof had to be jacked up with the grey slates in place to effect the repair. It wasn't possible to use a crane. Ian found the answer in one of his old technical books. *"We purchased a thick cotton rope and made it into a loop which passed under the roof truss and over the top of another joist which we had taken onto the outside of the roof. The rope was soaked with water and wound tight, this caused the rope to shrink and raised the rotted joist sufficiently to allow us to effect the repair."* Roof maintenance takes up much of the time of Ian and his helpers Half a ton of lead has just been used to reroof one room. The original had lasted well over two hundred years. *"How do you think,"* he asks, *"they got such* enormous roof timbers so high without cranes?" He chuckles at the thought, "They built the roof first and jacked it up bit by bit as they built the walls underneath." Yes they certainly knew a lot that we've forgotten.

Hoghton Tower is open for public viewing between Easter Saturday and the last Sunday in October. Private parties are catered for at other times by arrangement (minimum 25). An increasingly popular place for weddings, balls and corporate funtions, plus steam rallies, car launches and a host of other functions, it's good to know that Hoghton Tower is in such capable hands. For details of visits, functions or joining the Friends of Hoghton Tower, ring 01254 852986.

NICKED 'NICK'

Alan and Les Bond (Accrington)

The Town Hall clock struck ten to two
one dark December neet
A lonely policeman traipsed up brew
upon his frozen beat

His hands were dead inside his gloves
His ears and nose were blue
His feet were froze inside his shoes
His assets frozen too

A noise from off a nearby roof
made t'frozzen Policeman stop
In time to see a man emerge
from out a chimbley top

It made him feel elated
His thoughts began to soar
He'd been a policeman 20 years
never caught a thief before

So he scammered up a drainpipe
and then without a pause
He shouted "your arrested,
dressed up like Santa Claus"

The burglar is upset at this
"You can't nick me" he sings
"I'm really Father Christmas
and I'm giving all these things"

The Policeman laughed until he cried
"Oh yes I can and worse,
I'm charging you with trespassing
and burglary in reverse"

Incidents on the County's Early Highways

Early local newspapers record details about robberies that occured locally 200 years and more ago. Many seem to have remained inconclusive regarding the whereabouts of the offenders and their ill-gotten gains. Being a *'Gentleman of the Road'* was a particularly dangerous pastime because the death penalty was a certainty for those proved guilty. Hanging was the usual verdict just for the theft of a letter in the post, but from 1848 this was often commuted to *'transportation to the Colonies'*, usually Australia.

Larceny by Servants

On his usual journey from Lancaster to Preston, carrying mail as a postboy, on Tuesday 15th May 1722, William Johnson, aged 19, ran away with the sum of £50, leaving his boots, whip and horn lying in the road. Notices were issued branding him a robber, and rewards (£5) were offered by the Preston Postmaster, Richard Myers, to anyone who would secure the culprit. Further amounts of £40 were prescribed by Act of Parliament, and £200 by the General Post Office, but I have found no record of any arrest.

On 12th August 1848, *'The Lancaster Gazette'* reported that at the Assize, John Bickerstaff, Postman between Glasson and Lancaster, was sentenced to be transported for seven years for embezzling a letter given into his charge.

Early Morning Robbery

At 5 a.m. on the morning of 29th December 1799, a postboy carrying mails on horseback was stopped between Wigan and Chorley by a man on foot, who struck the boy with a sword and pulled him off his horse. This the robber mounted and rode away with all the mail in bags. This mail had left Liverpool for Lancaster on the 28th December, and the letters contained two bills for Thomas Rawlinson and Co. of Lancaster for £693 and £549. The usual rewards produced no known result. It is not clear if compensation was due or paid to Rawlinsons.

A notice was issued from the General Post Office in London on 3rd March 1800, announcing that the Postboy carrying Mails on horseback for Preston, Lancaster, Kendal and Carlisle, was stopped at 2 pm near Warrington. The robber made off with all the bags. Banknotes to the value of £260 were lost, and a reward offered of £200. It is not clear if the men charged at the Lancaster Lent Assizes with a mail robbery near Warrington were the criminals connected with that specific case, but the ring-leader, James Weldon, was found guilty of robbing the mails. He was hanged, and his body was encased in iron bands, covered in pitch, and gibbeted by the side of the road between Wigan and Ashton-in-Makerfield as a deterrent to others. The sentence awarded to John Burn and John Reddy, Welden's partners in crime, is not recorded.

At the Reins

On the 7th November 1811, the *'Lancaster Gazette'* reported that Thomas Backhouse of Lancaster, coach driver, was fined £5 for being intoxicated whilst driving the mails . Did he fall asleep? Did he drive off the road? Or could he not walk when he arrived in Lancaster? It is probable that he drove at a reckless speed causing his passengers to complain. The pre-occupation with speed was a constant problem due to the poor road surfaces, and because competition between the coach proprietors provided opportunities for drivers to attempt to shave the very tight schedules published in their timetables. Few major accidents were reported in the local papers. One of the first was on Friday 4th April 1823. It took place at the old Penwortham Bridge as two competing coaches travelling from Liverpool came down the long steep hill towards Preston at a great pace. They turned right towards the bridge, but neither would give way. The '**North Briton**' and the '**Robert Burns**' collided as they both turned sharply left to cross the old bridge. Damage and severe injuries were caused when one of the coaches turned over on to its side at the bridge entrance.

On Saturday 7th November 1818, the *'Preston Chronicle'* reported that the '**Bang Up**' coach from Manchester to Blackburn was overturned by coming into contact with the wheel of a wagon being overtaken. Most of the 9 or 10 outside passengers received severe bruising.

Periods of Refreshment

Despite the heavy uniforms and greatcoats worn by drivers and guards, the inclement weather on occasions was sufficiently bad to cause warm drinks to be taken at the inn where the change-over of drivers was arranged. Delays may well have tempted drivers to fortify themselves excessively at take-over points against long delays due to snow, gales or floods, so that subsequent actions on the road might give cause for alarm and concern among the passengers.

John Langhorne, of Lancaster, was reported in the *'Preston Chronicle'* of 31st October 1818 to have been fined £5 the previous week for being intoxicated whilst driving one of the public stage coaches between Garstang and Lancaster, and thereby causing danger to the passengers. Probably the coach concerned was the '**Royal Lancaster**' run by Thomas Cooper and Co. of Preston, which was advertised to leave Preston from the Castle Inn, Market Place, at 8 p.m. daily, and due into Lancaster at 11 p.m.. A longer wait than usual for the coach to arrive at Garstang's Royal Oak Hotel where the change of horses would be made may have been John's undoing that night.

Thomas Taylor was convicted, according to the *'Preston Chronicle'* on 11th November 1815, of driving the '**Price Regent**' coach in a manner so as to endanger the lives of the passengers and fined £10.

John Battersby, before the same magistrate, was fined a like amount for a similar offence whilst driving the '**Liverpool Light Post Coach**' on Wednesday 8th November 1815. The newspaper added that *"...we trust that these convictions may have the effect of preventing the present dangerous practice of racing adopted by drivers of stage-coaches upon the roads, but which we fear is carried to such an extent as to require interference of the legislature in passing an Act to inflict the punishment of imprisonment on the offender."*

BARTHOLOMEW BRETHERTON OF RAINHILL

The profit and prayers of Bartholomew Bretherton transformed the medieval hamlet of Rainhill into a bustling Victorian village.

It was just a ten mile journey from the *Saracen's Head*, Liverpool to the *Rainhill Tavern*. You can still see the milLestone on the humped-back and skew railway bridge near *'Kendrlck's Cross'*. When the turnpike to Warrington was opened in May 1760, the Tavern stood by the toll gate. Stage coach passengers clamoured for ale and food to warm themselves after the first three hour stage of their journey from Liverpool.

A motorist swooping over the bridge today into the narrow main street of Rainhill village would be unaware of the skew bridge, or the milestone. He might know of the Locomotive Trials of 1829 and the story of The Rocket but probably nothing of the growth of Rainhill in the preceding seventy years.

The *Saracen's Head*, owned by Bartholomew Bretherton, was for many years the principal coaching inn in Liverpool. Alas, the inn was a victim of the surge of Victorian development during the town's mid-nineteenth century boom. The Municipal Buildings now occupy the site. The *Rainhill Tavern* did, however, survive the ravages of time and, though often restored and refurbished, it continues to dominate the main street. Its name changed to the *Victoria Hotel* in honour of the young Queen, who visited the village on her way to Liverpool in 1851. Residents were not amused, therefore, when earlier this year a brewery replaced the head of the Queen on the pub sign with a giant plum. Civic and community leaders complained so vigorously that the brewery was compelled to restore the portrait of the Queen.

The Early Years

Raynhull existed as an agricultural community before the Norman Conquest. In the thirteenth century two separate communities grew up: the Windle family settled at the Manor House to the south-east and the Molyneux family at Rainhill Hall (now the Old Hall) to the south-west of the modern village. There was no church for either community: worshippers would travel to Prescot and, later, Portico for services.

That remained the position for six centuries until the Warrington road through Prescot, Rainhill, Bold and Sankey, became an impassable mud-pile in the late eighteenth century. The growth of Liverpool and its close commercial associations with London and Manchester demanded better communication links. The rutted roads made it impractical to carry heavy goods over long distances; wherever possible, shippers sent them by canal.

T'stage coach is a-comin'

The journey from Liverpool to London in those days involved a long ride on horseback or waggon to Warrington. There, travellers would meet the thrice-a-week stage coach service and the journey might take a week. Coaches had been introduced to England in 1564 from

70

Hungary. By 1672 there were still only six stage coaches operating in Britain: they all ran from London and only during the summer months. The destinations, York, Chester, Exeter, Oxford, Dover and Plymouth, did not include Liverpool, despite its expansion after the Restoration. Both Manchester and Warrington developed coach links with London before Liverpool, partly because the Dee and Mersey rivers were in the way, but mostly because of the state of the Warrington road.

A Copper Carriageway

Slag from the local copperworks strengthened the track when the newly widened road was opened in 1760. This made it durable for the heavier traffic that would now pass over it. Very quickly traffic to and from Liverpool increased and stage and mail coach operations would soon begin.

B.B.

When the first service between Liverpool and London opened through Rainhill and Warrington a year later, passengers had the comfort of a stage coach along the entire route for the first time. The single journey aboard **The Flying Machine** cost half-a-crown and took three days. Coaching continued to expand and improve for the next seventy years thanks to astute businessmen like Bartholomew Bretherton.

Bretherton was one of four brothers, all coach proprietors in Liverpool. Bartholomew's business, which operated from the *Saracen's Head* and the *Angel* in Dale Street, prospered better than the others, so much so that by 1832 he owned 20 of the 100 mail and stage coaches leaving Liverpool. At its peak the yellow livery was prominent on the road with services to Manchester fourteen times and London four times a day. The advertised journey-time to the *'Swan with Two Necks'* in Charing Cross, London, was twenty-three hours. It was unnecessary to change coach but the first change of horses took place at the *'Ship Inn'*, Rainhill, one mile further on from the Tavern.

Forward Planning

As early as 1804, Bretherton began to buy land nearby. He stabled a third of his stock of 700 horses there, and a third more at The Old Roan at Aintree and the remainder at Parr, north-east of St. Helens. By 1807 he was living in the neighbourhood and in 1824, when he owned much of the surrounding land, he built 'Rainhill House'. This remained in the family many years after his death, when the Society of Jesus bought it and established 'Loyola Hall', a retreat to the present day.

Bretherton understood the risk that the coming of the railway in 1830 posed. A dispute between canal owners and the merchants of Manchester and Liverpool accelerated the development of the infant technology. The resulting closure of the canals prevented cotton, timber and coal reaching their destination in Manchester. The railways provided swifter and cheaper transportation but the effect on passenger travel was an unexpected bonus.

Eager to reassure his regular clientele, Bretherton raced his coach the **Venture** against one of the first Manchester-bound trains. The **Venture** won the race by twenty minutes so delaying the inevitable decline. The rail link with London was not completed until 1838, but the businessman could see the writing on the wall. He sold much of his business to a competitor, investing instead in the railways. The residue of Bretherton's coach business was still operating in 1843, but he retired to his estate shortly afterwards and died there in 1857.

Some Early Lancashire Acts

In 1950, the County Archivist, Reginald *'Reg'* Sharpe France, (To whom our county owes a debt of gratitude beyond measure for the work he did in preserving records relating to many facets of our history) compiled a list of Lancashire-related Acts of Parliament he had encountered covering the years 1415 to 1800. He picked on that starting date because that was the earliest date he was aware of which mentioned Lancashire in a statute. It was one *'touching Abbots and Priors being suitors to Courts Baron in Lancashire and Yorkshire'* and was passed in the 3rd year of the reign of Henry V.

However, later research (1969) by a group of librarians under the guidance of Sidney Horrocks of Manchester's City Library unearthed another half-dozen Acts which specifically mentioned Lancashire being passed before the 1415 one.

The very first such Act was, as might be expected of one passed just two hundred years after the Norman Invasion (1266), in Latin. The *'Statutum de Scaccario'* includes references to the Sherrif of Lancashire. Today's Sherrifs can see an original copy of that statute in the City Library and in Chetham's Library, Manchester, in Stockport Library and at the County Record Office, Bow Lane, Preston. (Which came about through Sharpe France's efforts on our behalf) Amongst the others pre-1415 were ones excluding Lancashire from certain Weights and Measures legislation; one prohibiting the taking of salmon from *'Lone, Wyre, Mersee and Rybbul'* and all other waters in the county at certain times of year; and one declaring that Liverpool was one of the ports from which people may embark on a foreign voyage.

Horrocks' group, the Joint Committee on the Lancashire Bibliography, stopped declaring these Acts at the year 1957, at which date they had recorded 3,665 of them. This was before the computer age, so imagine the weight of the card index.

In his list, Sharpe France gathered 306 Acts. He categorised them under 15 headings:- bridges, canals, drainage, etc.. By far the greatest category was that dealing with matters affecting named people. There were 94 of these, including one of 1664 *'An Act for restoring Sir Charles Stanley in blood'* and one of 1685 *'An Act for rectifying certain errors and mistakes in the marriage settlement of Sir Charles Hoghton'*.

In the years following Sharpe France's cut-off date of 1800, over three thousand (to 1957) Acts were passed, many of them dealing with the towns which had grown up in the county. They touched on matters such as municipal nuisance, improvements, streets, water, gas, policing and finance. A separate set of Acts were passed to cover the coming of railways. From 1825 onwards, railway Acts became increasingly more common. Their numbers rocketed (sorry about that) up in the 1840s.

In the passing of these Acts can be traced the history of Lancashire itself, as bodies sought to acquire lawful authority to act in circumstances which were arising almost daily in an age of industrial revolution and which were not covered by the existing laws of the land. Such local and private Acts continue to be placed on the Statute Book of Great Britain. Others have made Blackpool, Blackburn and Warrington *'unitary authorities'*. Is history turning in a circle?

Trojans in the Mersey

by Eric Holt

It would be hard to imagine a link between the heroes of Homer's epic poem, '*The Illiad*', and the Port of Liverpool, but in the 1950s and 60s there was such a connection. It was in the fact that the ships of the Mersey-based Blue Funnel Line were all named after the legendary Greeks. This was the idea of Alfred Holt, founder of the Alfred Holt Company, owners of the Blue Funnel Line. As the name implies the ship's funnels were a distinctive blue with a black top emerging from the casing.

Names such as **Ajax, Ixion, Menelaus, Cyclops, Agamenon**, and others recalling the glory days of Troy became well known to me. I worked for a Bolton company as a shipping clerk. One of the areas to where we shipped was the Far East, the main destination of the Blue Funnel fleet.

Alfred Holt, who died in 1911, entered the shipping business in 1853. Being an engineer and a single-minded perfectionist it was natural that he should set a very high standard for any vessel owned by the company. So much so that '*Holt's class*' standard became second to none. It even surpassed *Lloyd's A1*, which had previously been recognised as the ultimate. Over the years the '*A1*' mark had been taken to be the best. '*Holt's class*' was better.

Although there were larger vessels sailing from Liverpool, notably the Cunard passenger liners, the Blue Funnel ships were always a favourite. Their distinctive styling and the fact that they sailed to exotic Pacific ports made them special. Between 1853 and 1960 the fleet totalled 294 ships. Little wonder that they became so much a part of the Mersey scene. World War 2 took a great toll of the Blue Funnel fleet. In it 41 ships were lost, almost half the total complement of 88. Ships were attacked in the Atlantic, the Pacific, the Indian Ocean, and even between Algiers and Gibraltar. No seas were safe. After the war, re-building began, and soon Blue Funnel regained its place as the most important cargo line between Europe and the Far East.

Nowadays, container ships have very little charisma. With their uncluttered decks stacked Lego-like with huge boxes they are rather like floating lorries. The Blue Funnel ships had style. In their own way they complimented the heroes such as Achilles, Ullyses, Jason, and other Homeric figures after whom they were named. One ex-shipping man remembers them with affection.

S.S.Alcinous steaming into Liverpool, her blue funnel apparent, even in a black & white photograph.
photo: John & Marion Clarkson, Longton.

GRANDAD'S FIND

When I was a little lad, my grandad used to meet me outside the Roxy Cinema every Saturday afternoon. He never had much money and it must have been a strain on his seven and sixpence disability pension to take us both there even though it cost four pence for the pair of us. Every Saturday at ten to two he'd be there in the same place outside the *'Flicks'* near the forthcoming attractions poster, leaning on his crutch, wearing his best cap and his highly polished clog. I once asked him why he only had one leg, and his reply was, *"Well I lost one."* A man of few words, my Grandad. I remember thinking how do you lose a leg? Do you wake up one morning to find that you are only taking up half the space in your pyjama bottoms? Are you sat there having tea and you reach down to pull your stockings up to find your leg has gone? I never asked him again. Whenever I asked my mum about it all she ever said was, *"The War."* I used to think well it couldn't have been much of a war if people go round losing legs and things, and if they did they wouldn't be much use to anyone would they? Anyway there I am waiting outside the Roxy and no Grandad yet. I always liked to get to the cinema early, I mean you need a bit of time to throw orange peel at each other, and we liked to do a lot of shouting, I don't mean shouting at Grandad: nobody shouted at my Grandad. We also had a lot of running around to do, up and down the aisles, a lot of jerseys to pull and a lot of seats to crawl under. More fun than watching the flicks.

Intervals were best. We used to start imitating characters we'd just seen and it could get quite rough. If it had been **The Three Stooges**, Larry would give Curly a clout on his bald head and it would make a bone-cracking sound; when we did it to each other all it did was hurt like hell. Cowboy films would have us galloping around on imaginary horses slapping our backsides in place of our pretended mounts.

Today, Grandad was unusually late. *"Where's my bloody Grandad?"* I muttered to myself. I were right good at swearing to myself and was looking forward to doing it out loud one day. I didn't have a watch but I knew it must have been after two o' clock because everybody had gone in. So I set off to walk in the direction that I knew Grandad would take. As I got half way over the iron bridge, I saw him leaning on the metal work supporting himself with his crutch.

"Hello Grandad, what's up?" *"By Gum, lad, I'm right glad to see you. I knew you would come to find me."* *"Is there summat wrong, Grandad?"* *"Nay lad, there's nowt wrong except I can't bend down."* *"Well what's wrong wi that Grandad?"* *"I'll show you what's wrong wi that,"* and he moved the end of his crutch to reveal there on the pavement a bright shiny half-crown piece. *"Pick that up lad and give it to me."*

Two and sixpence was big money in those days and I knew my Grandad would have stood there as long as it took rather than leave it for someone else to find. By the time we got to the Roxy we'd missed episode 24 of **The Mark of Zorro** and **The Three Stooges in Egypt**, but Laurel and Hardy were still to come. Later, at home, when my mum had put my tea on the table, I didn't feel hungry. Three choc-ices and two bags of crisps had done for me. As for Grandad, spending money was as great a pleasure as finding it. Even with my choc-ices, he still had enough for a couple of extra pints that Saturday night.

THE TRAIL OF THE LAST WOLF

The legend of the last wolf is often mentioned in guide books to the Lake District. Its source is a poem from the *'Annals of Cartmel'*. There are many stories about the last wolf in England. Like Arthurian legends, they crop up in any region where the folk memory is long. The most recent dates only from 1906. We are indebted to Mrs. Jerome Mercier for drawing together the various strands of the legend and putting them along with the poem in a slim volume that was published in Grange-over-Sands five hundred years or so after the event.

Most of the accounts of the legend agree that it was a proclamation issued by King Edward the First, who was no stranger to Cumbria (he died there in 1307), that prompted the hunt. Edward reigned from 1272 to 1307, so we can put the wolf episode into this time period. The Holy Land fell in 1291, so this could narrow the field somewhat, as, in the legend, John Harrington, the main protagonist has returned from the Holy Land where it was feared he had fallen in battle.

The trouble starts when the wolf, whose lair by tradition was in Borrowdale, came down through to the Cartmel Peninsula seeking food and a mate. *'The great wolf which is to be hunted at last'*, suggests a sport was made out of the event and that the wolf was terrorising the townships of Cartmel was a flimsy excuse, as wolves usually stay away from humans.

Edgar Harrington, the Master of Wraysholme Tower, a Pele tower near Allithwaite, offered up the prize of the hand of Adela, his ward, in marriage. John Harrington, estranged son of Edgar, took up the King's challenge as did a Red Cross Knight of Leyburne. John had assumed the title 'Delisle' and had caught the eye of fair Adela.

John Harrington features largely in Furness history. His tomb can be seen in Cartmel Priory Church. It is perhaps because he was such a colourful character that legends grew around him. When he died he owned properties in Cumberland, Westmorland and Lancashire. Sir Edgar's Master of Hounds, 'Old Hubert', was said to lead the hunt. They first went to Humphrey Head, a raised headland that juts out into the sandy wastes of Morecambe Bay, but they found that the wolf had fled to the lands of Holker, now famous for its Motor Museum and Gardens. The trail then led to Roudsea Woods, now a Nature Reserve.

The wolf made good ground swimming across the Leven, then proceeded up the Crake Valley and along the banks of Coniston. From there, he headed back eastwards through Esthwaite and then crossed Windermere. The fortitude of this creature must have been quite something, though we do not know the time scale of the chase. The wolf now followed the River Winster to Witherslack, crossed Meathop Moss through Eggerslack, a wooded fell side on the eastern flank of Hamps Fell, down through what is now Grange-over-Sands and back to Humphrey Head. There the cornered animal did the noble thing, jumping off the cliff, followed allegedly by Sir John's white Arab steed. Sir John duly married Adela in the cave on Humphrey Head and they lived happily for many years.

Her eyes are closed with mortal dread
And 'ere a look they steal,
The wolf and arab both lie dead,
And scathless stands De Lisle.

The wolf's fleece was said to be preserved at 'Atterpile', now known as 'Castle Head', a house built on an outcrop to the east of Eggerslack.

Believe what you will. Sir John's wife was actually Joan of Dacre so the record tells us, but the tale is not wholly unbelievable and it is possible to visit most of the places associated with the legend. Arnside Tower also features in the legend too, but **Wolf House**, near Silverdale, has only a tenuous connection. The coat of arms of the family who built it had a wolf on their crest.

So, gentle reader, if you venture on Humphrey Head and the mist slowly draws in across the Bay, you may feel that eyes watch you from the woods. Do not fear, but have pity on the soul of the last wolf still searching for its mate.

ROSSENDALE REVIEWED

We publish without comment a letter sent to the '*Sheffield Daily Telegraph*' in November 1878. The '*Bacup Times*' repeated it within a few days, but we haven't enquired as to what their readers thought about it!

The Forest of Rossendale

"There is a painful absence of 'forest' or anything approaching thereto. The eye roves over bleak, barren moors, or along bare ugly hills, searching in vain for vestiges of the alleged 'forest'.

Take a birds eye view from the highest eminence and what do you see most of all is - STONE. It crops up everywhere. Rossendale is still in the stone age, nor is there any expectation that it will ever emerge therefrom.

Mountainous dirt heaps - yawning quarries - lines of flag-laden trucks.

It is a dreary work-a-day place, in which a depressed, unintelligent population makes shift to exist in a variety of disagreeable ways. The people of the 'forest' are gaunt, tall, or lumpy and squat, with an expression on their faces as if their minds were constantly dwelling on the idea of suicide, or as if they had made a wager with someone that they would never look pleasant in their lives, and were determined to win.

Yet when the 'forrester' opens his mouth (or rather when he is in the humour to speak, for his mouth is ever open) he utters, not wise and witty words, but instead rolls out oaths and curses, which his wonderful dialect happily half conceals.

This is one of the reasons why the 'forest' offers a fine field for missionary labour. As a mission field, Rossendale has attractions which in Africa do not exist. The missionary here may go about, almost with the certainty that he will not be eaten. In the very worst times, when half the population was being slowly starved on parish allowance, a missionary would only be 'summat to eat'. This fact secures him immunity. Were he 'Summat to sup' the matter would be different.

The 'factory hands' are an entirely different class. They are as insignificant physically as the 'brownbacks' (quarrymen) are prodigious. Cadaverous faces, sunken eyes, leaden looks and general ricketiness - such, and their clogs, are the distinguishing peculiarities of the mill-workers. They are strangely ignorant.

They have not enough character to make them interesting as a study, but are just a dull stolid, depressed class, about whom no one would care to concern himself.

Of the outside world they know little, and care less - being wholly wrapped up in themselves. Their life, reflected by their newspapers, is one of beer-drinking and tea-drinking, both in extremes.

The valley is chiefly inhabited by two classes - 'factory hands' and 'brownbacks'.

The 'brownback' is a picturesque, if not romantic being. He swears with perhaps more real grace, vigour and effectiveness than any other person whatever. Everything about him is massive, but for his understanding. His dress is primitive, consisting of a 'slop' (or overall) a red handkerchief and a hairy cap. If he wants to be particular he adds trousers, but these when first introduced were considered luxuries, and avoided by the steady conservative ones. The 'brownback' is engaged in the 'delphs' or quarries, and partakes of the roughness of the material among which he works. When not blasting on his employers behalf, he is 'blasting' on his own personal account. He might be put forward to out-swear, out-drink and out-eat any competition. He is indifferent as to his lodging and will sleep anywhere. A saint existed in the old time in Cyprus who allowed dirt to accumulate on his body till he was encased in it as a suit of armour. The 'brownback' imitates the saint largely not for the love of sanctity, but for love of ease.

The hours away from the delph he considers time for drinking beer, or if he has no money, to stand at street corners, envying those who have.

He fights policemen, and maltreats his wife, if he owns a slave of that description.

There are some churches and chapels, and clergymen and ministers, hence it is evident that the place is regarded as civilised and christian.

The Rossendale Valley might well be called the 'Valley of Tears' in respect to the spitting rain which continues 23 out of the 24 hours, the odd hour being devoted to comical attempts on the part of the sun to 'get up a shine'. The clouds from all quarters make a point of dissolving immediately over the unfortunate district. As a consequence the earth is sodden and soaked. The drenched natives are for ever looking as if they had by accident tumbled into a canal and just scrambled out.

Nature has hardly acted fairly by the Rossendalers; since she gave them such a climate, she ought in conscience to have made them waterproof."

77

JOURNEY'S END

Like pilgrims to th' appointed place we tend.
The world's an inn, and death the journey's end.

John Dryden

Today we can see all the world news at the flick of a switch. Do we ever wonder how events were recorded in bygone days? Newspapers have been available for the best part of two centuries, but how do we know what happened in previous times? Parliamentary papers, diaries and family papers are rich in information, but they are all too few. Nineteenth century historians such as Edward Baines - editor of the *Leeds Mercury*, and William Robertson, reporter on the *Rochdale Observer* were newspaper men first and historians secondly. They relied in the main on oral history for their knowledge of events - sometimes resulting in inaccurate, embroidered accounts.

Veracity from the Vicar

There is however another irrefutable source of information - the church registers. Many entries record only the bare facts, but in the time of Thomas Bellas, curate at St.Chad's Rochdale, the comments which are added to the burial records give us an insight into many aspects of daily life.

Thomas Bellas came as curate to Rochdale in 1770, At first he received only the 'surplice' fees (approx. £50 per annum) but in the time of Dr. Drake he received an additional £34-13-4. He was also rector of Holdenby in Northamptonshire although he never resided there. He was a popular clergyman mingling with poor and monied classes alike. However his lifestyle was not exactly suited to his vocation and this was presumably the reason for his undoing. He was the bishop's surrogate for marriages and his accounts were found to be defective by the Commissioners of Stamps. In 1805 he left Rochdale very precipitately, never to return. Robertson records that he was later seen in Madeira. Who says crime does not pay?

Commenting from the Graveside

His comments betray a keen eye for the newspaper headline. No doubt had he lived a little later he may have chosen this as his vocation. He was not fitted for the vocation he chose. He records on 20th November 1786 *"Richard Haigh of Lowershore. gentleman, perished through the inclemency of the weather."* On 30th December 1791 Charles Hill, a weaver *"starved to death in the snow."* On 17th April 1792 Mary Kay of Trough *"was killed by lightening."* From such entries we have some idea of the weather conditions of the time.

Working conditions are also illustrated by such as the entry of 21st October 1791. Edmund Butterworth of Well' i' th' Lane weaver was killed by an engine and on 27th January 1793 David, son of Samuel Cryer, Heybarn was *"killed by a carding mill"*. Conditions in the early factories were poor and many such accidents would occur. Children were employed at a very early age and for very long hours. These conditions were eventually recognised by the Ten Hours Bill.

Conditions in the mines remained very dangerous and it was not until 1842 that a Royal Commission was set up to investigate them. On 18th November 1784, James, son of Thomas Lees of College Houses, collier was killed in an accident in a coalpit. (Children often worked along side their parents, hauling bogies etc.) An entry for 9th February 1791 records the death of John Lord, Cloughbottom, a collier, in an accident. Such accidents were common. On 9th March 1794 the deaths of two children in the coalpits are recorded. Elizabeth, daughter of Mary Whitham ,Great Howarth and James, son of Samuel Whipp, also of Great Howarth both seem to have perished in the same accident. Poor little children working in the darkness of a coalpit for as long as fourteen hours a day. Little wonder accidents happened and their brief lives were brought to an untimely end.

Dyeing and Dying

The process of dyeing seems to have been equally hazardous. James Gibson a dyer is recorded on 1st November 1792 as having been *"scalded to death in a dyepan at Town Mill"*. On 25th June 1794 Thomas, son of James Clegg of Milnrow, dyer, met his end in the same way. The building of the canal in 1794 also claimed its victims. On 12th December 1794 Thomas Holt of Church Style was killed by accident in the canal This would be the first of many such accidents.

Suicides, murders and accidental but lurid deaths are recorded alike. On 5th January 1784 Sarah Matthew of Pitts, spinster is reported to have poisoned herself. On 21st March 1794 Benjamin Oldham of Church Lane, a hatter, is recorded as having *"hanged himself (Lunatic)"*. Prolonged exposure to working with lead in the manufacture of hats literally drove them mad - hence the expression *'mad as a hatter'*.

On 25th April 1792 John Howarth, an innkeeper was reported as *"killed and manslaughtered"*. Nothing seems to change! The Demon Drink is not omitted. On 29th May 1784 Thomas Deign of Inghams, husbandman, is said to have died *"by excessive drinking of spirituous liquers"*, and on 4th May 1793, John Fletcher, a sawyer, by *"phyrie and drinking"*. If the hazards of working life did not kill you there was always the chance that some dread disease would. On 13th April 1790 a stranger, his name unknown, *"died from the smallpox"* in Rochdale. Imagine the panic that death would cause!

Seventy Plus

Some seemed to have survived against all odds. There are entries such as that of 23rd July 1790 of Robert Chadwick, clothier, who died aged 94. There is also Mary Lord of Hungerhill, widow, who died at 100 in 1791. Frances Crossley of Blackwater, widow, died aged 108 and on 15th May 1797 James Wild, inmate of Hollinworth workhouse, died aged 104. These survived considerably longer than the 'alloted span'.

A Question Mark

To the credit of Thomas Bellas one headline which does **not** appear in the records is the entry recording the death of his second wife by her own hand. There is merely a bald entry of her burial in the registers.

The numerous entries such as these which appear in the registers give us a good insight into the daily life of Rochdale. Our grateful thanks to Thomas Bellas, frustrated reporter and failed cleric.

WHIT MONDAY IN COLNE

In the years immediately after the war, Whitsuntide was still one of the main events in the religious and social calendar of Colne. On Whit Monday, there would be a procession of Christian Witness in the town known as *'walking'*. All the non-conformist congregations assembled on the Market Ground. There was no shortage of nonconformists in Colne. There were Methodists of the Wesleyan, Independent, and Primitive persuasion, Baptists, Congregationalists, Unitarians, Christadelphians and Inghamites. A local schism among the Inghamites led to there being the *'Top of Winewall Inghamites'* and the *'Bottom of Winewall Inghamites'* each with their own chapel. If there had been militant extremist non-conformists they would have had their headquarters in Colne.

Ne'er the Twain Shall Meet

The Church of England did not join with the chapel folk for the walk. They had a service in the church yard and then watched the non-conformists' parade from their elevated vantage point before beginning their own, smaller, but more exclusive, procession. If the dissenters were ordinary working folk, the Anglicans had aspirations to be the upper crust of small town life. By tradition, the church had an Oxford M.A. as its vicar. The non-conformist preachers were local men.

My mother had been brought up as a Methodist at the Bethel Chapel and her grand father had been a lay preacher at the Primitive Methodists. However, on moving house to

Colne's Whit Walk in Albert Road, May 1950. Colne Borough Band leading the way followed by nineteen churches and fourteen Sunday school parades.

nearer the centre of town, my mother switched allegiance to the Anglicans. She took me to her confirmation classes while I was only three or four years old. In the old Norman church, the ladies of the class sat in awe of the rector, the aptly named Mr Macvicar. I fidgeted with boredom, playing with the hassocks and hymn books.

Spectacular

As a small child, I found the main procession on Whit Monday the most fun. From the church yard we would hear the strains of hymns long before the parade came into view as it reached the Town Hall. Colne Borough Band led the procession. If the mayor was in the parade, he wore his chain of office and was accompanied by the mace bearer. Each chapel had a banner, supported by two poles, which bore its name and a colourful picture on a biblical theme. Guy ropes were attached to the top of each pole to steady the banner against gusts of wind. It was a privilege to support the banner. The Salvation Army Band members wore their traditional black uniforms with red trim. They had a flag bearer, who was by far the tallest man in Colne at nearly seven feet. He was very impressive as he marched at the front of their detachment with the flag-pole in a leather socket at his waist. The Anglicans thought that some of the Salvation Army tunes such as *'Shall we Gather at the River'* and *'What a Friend we have in Jesus'* were a little too jaunty compared with their hymns and psalms. *'Onward Christian Soldiers'* was one of my favourites. At length, the procession passed and the sound of the bands receded.

The Anglicans then walked in silence through the main street of soot-stained buildings as far as the top of Skipton Road. A choir boy carrying a cross led the procession. He was followed by the vicar, church wardens, and the sidesmen bearing their sticks of office. Behind them came the Scouts and Guides, Sunday School classes, the Youth Club, and the rest of the congregation. It was an awesome experience to walk in the middle of the road, seeing the spectators and special constables lining the kerb.

Our procession ended at the Sunday School Rooms in Exchange Street, where there were trestle tables set out with refreshments. The scones that awaited us were so full of baking soda that they made me thirsty. The only drink available was strong tea, which had been stewing in the urn for half an hour just in case we finished early. The slightest sip of it curled my tongue. In the afternoon there were the Sports. The Methodists had their own field a good mile from the town centre near Smith Lane. The Anglicans used the recreation ground near Alkincoates Park. Sunday School children competed in various events such as the egg and spoon and sack races. Teenage boys, in their oldest clothes, tried to climb the greasy pole. It was at such an event, when I was three, in 1948, that I first tasted candy floss. Father snapped me with his box Brownie as I struggled with the fluffy confection. It must have been a cold day, as the photograph shows me wearing a Harris Tweed coat with a velvet collar.

(This article based on one which first appeared in 'Lancashire History Quarterly')

PLAYTIME IN THE '30s

My brother an I grew up in Burnley, a typical Lancashire textile town, in the years prior to the Second World War. Our home was a two-up two-down house that stood in the shadow of the mills. During the school holidays in the summer months, every day was playtime. If it so happened that our parents were in a period of employment, we remained unsupervised during the day and consequently from time to time we suffered the wrath of neighbours when the street games became a little high-spirited. One such occasion was when a scene taken straight from a western movie showing at the local cinema was re-enacted in the back street. Our ranch, which was the back yard of the house, was under siege from a particularly militant band of Indians. My brother and myself were the sole survivors of a beleaguered outpost. The Indians, making their final assault had already penetrated the outer defences and were clambering over the roof of the outside lavatory. Alas, unlike the film, the expected cavalry had failed to arrive on time, so as a last-ditch stand, I took up a bucket that was half full of rainwater, and with a suitable amount of banging and shrieking, discharged the contents over the back yard wall.

Among the invaders, young Redskin Harry was no less agile than the rest, but mentally he was less alert. Instead of taking quick evasive action, he stepped forward and took the full force of my water canon. Parents duly returned home and then came the inevitable knock on the door. Harry's mother, who I considered was a little over-protective of her offspring, was particularly vocal when recounting the events of the day. Her threats carried conviction. During the weeks that followed I took good care to give her a wide berth, but whenever I caught sight of her it confirmed my opinion that she resembled a broody hen.

The 'Rec'

The official recreation ground was no more than a cinder-covered piece of spare land situated some distance from our home; consequently our play area was amid rows of terraced houses. Regular street traders became familiar figures. There was the **milkman** on his horse-drawn float who called twice a day to ladle fresh milk from his churn into jugs brought out into the street. There was scant regard for the bits of soot which were a permanent hazard when most homes were heated by coal fires.

These 3 rapscallions posed for a camera in 1935 before resuming their play in Collingwood Avenue, Blackpool - Jim Hunt, Jimmy Hoyle and Alan Hunt.

The **scissors grinder** was an occasional visitor who set up his barrow outside local mills and with his pedal-powered grinder did a brisk trade. From time to time the **chimney sweep** visited homes where the family was in employment. In the interest of economy, unemployed people set fire to their own chimneys. A rolled-up newspaper and a drop of paraffin was all that was required to get into business, but they first took care to note the whereabouts of the local constable who patrolled the streets on foot on a regular basis.

The **'rag chap'** ('recycling agent' in modern parlance) was daily seen pushing a pram piled high with a miscellany of discarded clothing. He made his presence known by a call that was immediately recognised by the locals. In return for old rags and woollen garments, he distributed yellow or white sandstones that were used to stripe the edge of the doorstep after the weekly ritual of *'mopping out'*.

The **'ice-cream chap'** had a practical approach. He rang his bell and conserved his vocal chords. Without doubt the most colourful character that called was **'Torpedo-Tommy'**. (A 'torpedo' is a pie not unlike in shape and content a Cornish pasty - Ed.) When he made his round in the evening, he carried a cloth-covered wickerwork basket over his arm, and from it he dispensed tasty morsels along with a lively banter seasoned with a touch of Irish brogue.

White made Black, Air made Blue

Each day brought variety. Monday was washday. From early morning, activities centred around *'dolly tubs'* and *'possers'*. Whenever washing was hung out to dry on lines suspended across the back street, all ball games were strictly forbidden. The washing line posed an inconvenience to all passing tradesmen, but a bane to the coal chap. Whenever the cry went out *"The coal chap is coming!"* we gathered around and awaited the time when things did not go according to plan. It was the usual practice for the lady of the house to use a long wooden prop to lift the clothes line clear whilst the coal cart passed beneath, but a freak gust of wind or a sudden impulsive move by the coal chap could lead to disaster. If the washline became entangled, the result would be black streaks across the newly-boiled whites - followed by a dickens of a row. After just such an incident, Mrs. Proud, who was normally a quiet well-spoken lady with impeccable manners, - **ERUPTED**. She poured out a torrent of abuse that eclipsed that of any hardened campaigner. Subjected to such a barrage, the coal chap's face, already begrimed, turned pink. A stream of invective flowed freely from the tongue of a normally demure housewife. The action was fast and furious; sparks flew. We revelled in the excitement. Barely pausing for breath, she continued to lambaste the offender with a seemingly endless string of colourful adjectives delivered without a single repetition. The coal chap beat a hasty retreat, but not before Mrs. Proud launched a parting shot that cast doubt on his parentage.

From a safe distance we could only stand and marvel at her command of the expletive.

83

OUR STAPLE INDUSTRY IS WINGING AHEAD

Even today, the world associates Lancashire with the cotton industry. The world is mistaken, for our leading employer by far in the county is now the aerospace industry.

We lead ~ Heads held high

Lancashire is way out in front in Great Britain, providing (1995 figures) 13% of all UK direct aerospace jobs, accounting for more than 20% of all aerospace production, and in the previous four years creating jobs and wealth 50% higher than the figures for the industry nationwide.

In the past decade, the industry has been the strongest performer of all the county's industries, helping to drive along the other sectors through the wages paid and wealth and jobs created as off-shoots.

Things have moved on a piece since this photo was taken in a Manchester factory in the mid-1930s.

Fly~past

Perhaps the story started in Preston, when, in the 1920s, the English Electric Company were building flying boats, but it certainly *'took off'* in the years of the re-armament drive before the Second World War. Our large engineering labour force was ideal for the factories started at Blackpool, Preston, Accrington, Lancaster, Burnley and (in White Rose land) Barnoldswick. These were created to *'shadow'* or duplicate the factories in the Midlands likely to become targets for German bombers.

The war over, production expanded at these and other factories - Chadderton, Trafford Park and Woodford (Cheshire). The success rate in world terms has been incredible. Here, work was done on developing the world's first jet engine, Sir Frank Whittle's W.2.B, and its successors to power the Canberra, Lightning, Provost, Strikemaster, Jaguar, Tornado and currently the Eurofighter and Hawk. Where else in the world does such a pedigree exist? Nowhere.

Big Names and Little Ones

The world has heard of our big-name employers: Rolls Royce and British Aerospace employ many thousands. So too do the myriad of small and medium-sized firms and companies in the industry. All these are together under an umbrella organisation - **The Consortium of Lancashire Aerospace (CLA)** was launched in 1993 by the industry itself to lobby, being *'dedicated to promoting and expanding the North West region's innovative aerospace and high technology engineering base by encouraging investment in the region and by marketing internationally the advanced infrastructure, in particular the region's outstanding technology and skill base'.*

Since then, the CLA has become a company limited by guarantee, working for the benefit of all the **143** companies it represents, encouraging and co-ordinating research and development and promoting exports globally. The world will hear more of Lancashire.

The Consortium represents aerospace companies based outside the present Lancashire County Council boundary. To the CLA, *Lancashire* means Lancashire. There are even a few companies in the fold from places outside the true county boundary.

In researching this piece, I have been greatly helped by Paul Hughes of the CLA and by John Longworth and Peter Kivell of the County Planning Officer's Department, County Hall, Preston. The CLA can be contacted on 1254 389222 (tel) or 389393 (fax).

☙❀❧

A view of Lancaster across the Lune from Skerton about 1937. Here is city hustle and bustle, packed 'buses, pedestrians aplenty and the convenience of a convenience in the foreground. Note that the gentlemen's portion is open to the elements.

photo: Ed Tyson collection.

A LANCASHIRE LAD DOES THE COUNTRY PROUD

When there's a job needing to be done, there's a Lancashire lad who will do it - even though the job is enormous.

For many years, Tony Rae, a sergeant in the Lancashire Constabulary stationed near Preston has had an interest in police history. About fifteen years ago, having taken a special interest in policemen who had been killed on duty, he decided to start recording those officers, male and female, and the circumstances of their death. Underlying every name was the fact that each had died for the good of the community they served.

The Enormity

Computer switched on, Tony started reading. He hasn't stopped since - every issue of *The Times* for 202 years, every issue of *Police Review* for 104 years, over 5,250 other magazines, over 100 books, *Hansard* for over a century - and much, much more.

Tony has hit a problem faced by all researchers into policing - records have been thrown away. Many forces have ceased to exist, mostly through amalgamation with larger bodies. In Lancashire alone, five borough forces ceased to exist in 1947, another dozen in 1969, followed by yet more re-organisation, and destruction of records, in 1974. Tony is working on a national scale.

As with all legal matters, Tony decided to work within a framework of definitions. He used the definitions of *'police officer'* and *'line of duty'* laid down by the leading official bodies, who recognise that there are several types of death; acts of violence of different sorts; accidental; natural; misadventure and 'unknown'.

Looking for help in researching, Tony found it in the *Police Federation*, the *Police Superintendents Association*, the *Association of Chief Police Officers* and the *National Association of Special Constabulary Officers*. Doors were opened throughout the country and enthusiasm for his project grew.

He has received funding (this is entirely a private research project), and his Chief Constable, Mrs. Clare, has afforded him some facilities to allow his project to continue. Tony is particularly proud of a handwritten note from her which says *"Well done Sgt. Rae"*.

Superintendent Richardson's finely-phrased gravestone in Layton Cemetery, Blackpool.
photo: A. Rae

I said the job was enormous. To date, Tony has logged over 3,000 deaths in the execution of duty since paid policemen appeared on our streets two hundred years ago. Sadly, a third of these are Northern Ireland officers.

Lancashire features all too often. Of particular note are the deaths of Superintendent Gerry Richardson, shot by a robber at Blackpool in 1971, the highest ranking officer in the record, and Policewoman Myra Waller, 24 years of age, was the first female officer to be killed on duty in peacetime when her car crashed whilst she was answering an emergency call at Lancaster in 1965.

Financial help has come from the *Police History Society* and the *Friends of the Metropolitan Police Museum*. A further boost to Tony's work, especially in recognising its value to the Police Sevice and the country as a whole, has come in a dedication by the *National Memorial Arboretum Appeal* to use his records as a Roll of Honour when the National Police Memorial being planned in Staffordshire is completed. This will have a plant for every officer listed, amongst an avenue of trees, one for every force past and present.

Alongside his researching, Tony has written about the Preston Borough Police Force, and he still finds time to lock people up. He is throwing a ray of light on names deserving of eternal sunshine. He is ensuring that **We Shall Not Forget**: Well done Sgt. Rae.

LETTERS TO THE EDITOR.

THE SANITARY CONDITION OF BELTHORN.

Sir.—It was with no small satisfaction that I read the bills distributed by the Tory candidates at the last Local Board election, making special mention of the necessary improvements required at Belthorn. I may say it was agreed upon by both parties in the village not to support any candidates who would not "go in" for the improvement of Belthorn with respect to water and a proper system of sewage. Now, what has become of those promises ; this item of the Tory programme? Nothing. True, they have frightened a few to put their closets on the tub system, but the worst still remain. We have still with us the liquid excreta in the open channels on the main roads ; we have still the little lakes of sewage and filth ; and we have still to be content with an impure water supply. It was with a great flourish of trumpets that members of the Board professed to have bought land for sewage tanks in front of the parsonage, and close by the garden wall or fence of the best house of the village. No doubt they hoped for some opposition to this site, so as to have some excuse for doing nothing ; but it is rather significant that those who professedly bought the land had come up to the annual tea at the Tory club, and, of course, speeches had to follow. Now, where are those rising hopes of the Tory party ? Have they done according to promise, or are they yet intending to do something?

In my opinion it is well for Belthorn that we have had such excessive rains this summer as we are at present comparatively free from sickness. But what think you, sir, of the following fact—that the man employed by the Local Board to cart away the excreta, &c., has nowhere to take it only on to his field, which is in close proximity to the village, so close indeed that I have seen it within twenty yards of the front and only door of one of the houses—a regular spread of *pure* excreta at the time two young men were lying in the house—one dying and the other dead.

It is with a feeling of deep disgust that I have written the above, for we have petitioned and sent deputations to the Board until we are weary, as well as having written to the Local Government Board and the County Medical Officer, and with no more success than you see. We are left "to stew in our own juice." Poor Belthorn ! But the rates are collected as usual. As a guarantee of the truth of what I have stated, and thanking you in anticipation for the insertion of this letter in your next issue, I subscribe myself

WM. HENRY YATES.

From the Accrington Observer,
3rd October 1891

87

PICKUP BANK SUNDAY SCHOOL OLD CHAPEL

High on the moors above Darwen stands a little chapel, special in many people's hearts. Pickup Bank Sunday School, known as Pickup Bank Old Chapel, has stood the test of time for many years.

Prior to 1821, Yate and Pickup Bank and Hoddlesden townships had no religious or educational facilities. There had been a building at Yate Bank which had been used as a Day School, but it never belonged to the Church of England. Up to 1816, local farmers were trustees of this building, but for many years afterwards it was not used, either as a Day School or Sunday School. Then, some Wesleyan Methodists, Messrs. Hough, Hillsborough and Thornber, came from Edgworth, and brought with them a number of families of the same religious persuasion, to work at their calico printworks at Dick Bridge. In 1821, they opened a Sunday School in a cottage house at 'Top o' the Meadow'. but the printworks closed and its owners left the neighbourhood. The Sunday School was closed and all activities were suspended. In 1826, the Independents of Lower Chapel took another cottage at 'Top o' the Meadow' and began a Sunday School. This was probably where Pickup Bank Old Chapel began.

There were a lot in the neighbourhood who could neither read nor write. Most of those who could had attended Sunday School and places of worship in Darwen. It became evident to those who were eductaed, that people in Hoddlesden and Yate and Pickup Bank had been neglected in religious and educational matters, so they decided to make amends. About 1828, Jeremy Hunt began a school for adults at 8 a.m. on Sunday mornings. This was carried on for a number of years and in 1834 the place was taken up by the Blackburn Academy, which made a grant of £10 a year towards the services. A pulpit, bible and hymn books were purchased by subscription, and 3s. 3d. was left as a balance after paying for these items. It was decided to make Hunt a present of the amount. He firmly declined to receive it for himself, saying: *"Well, give it to me and we will build a new chapel with it."* A meeting was called to consider this suggestion and £7 raised for the proposed building fund. Later this became £30.

Up and Running

In Spring 1834, they began to build a chapel: it took eighteen months to complete. Men dug out the foundations and did most of the building work free of charge. Stone was obtained locally for nothing. The ground rent for the site and burial ground was just 1 shilling per year. The chapel was opened on 5th November 1835, to the delight of the little community. In 1887, a fund was raised for a minister's house, but three years later this was transferred to the fund for a new chapel and school in Hoddlesden. Many people had moved down into Hoddlesden seeking work there. The access roads to the Pickup Bank Chapel were becoming more difficult and the older people could not make their way there, especially in the winter.

It was decided to concentrate on raising money for a new chapel in Hoddlesden, and in 1892 a mammoth bazaar was held in Darwen's Co-op Halls which raised £600. When a site at Hoddlesden had been chosed, building commenced in April 1899. In May 1900, the new chapel was opened at a cost of £3,600. £1,100 was still needed, so another bazaar was held. This cleared the debt and left some money in hand. Later, an organ was added.

The new chapel was opened by Alderman Lightbown of Darwen who praised the chapel workers for moving nearer the centre of population. The pastor of Bolton Road Congregational Church, Darwen, praised the workers and said that the building was: *"by far the most handsome building in Hoddlesden and far exceeds my expectations"*. The last service was held here on 28th December 1986, so the New Chapel had served the congregation for eighty-six years.

The New Chapel flourished for many years. There was the added bonus of a schoolroom and its accessibility made it popular. Looking through the records, many of the names remain constant throughout the years, both supporting the old chapel and the new. Harwood, King, Taylor, Walsh, Page, Yates, Wood, Hacking, Townsend, Cooper - these are but a few of the names of families who had held positions of respect and trust, since the old chapel was opened. Their heirs, it would appear, were willing to give service and devotion to both old and new chapels. Allan Cooper, the present chairman of Trustees, followed in his father's, grandfather's and great-grandfather's footsteps.

That grand old character *'Jem o' Rosins'* (James Townsend), was a stalwart. He was the first child to be baptised at the new chapel on 9th September 1900. His daughter, Marion Robinson, is a member of today's congregation. Misses Rachel and Jenny Harwood followed a long family tradition by becoming Sunday School teachers.

The new chapel in Hoddlesden served its purpose, yet, as if waiting in the wings, the old chapel looked down from the hillside above *'Old Rosin's Inn'*. Parishioners had not allowed it to fall into disrepair, and although there was no electricity or sewage, they still made a pilgrimage, three times a year, to hold services in the place their ancestors had loved. The old chapel remained virtually the same - flag floors, a huge old stone fireplace. Tilley lamps hanging from the beams, together with candles, provided the only lighting. The woodwork of the pulpit and pews was still polished by caring hands. The old chapel, drowsing on the hillside, seemed to know that one day it would have a new lease of life as a place of worship. Its graveyard was still the burying ground for many families.

In the 1970s and '80s, Hoddlesden expanded, new houses abounded, many peopled by those who worked in towns yet wanted to live in a rural setting. Sadly, the upkeep of the new chapel became too much for the dedicated band of workers and in 1986 it was decided to close it and concentrate on the old one. Cars made the old chapel more accessible and attractive. Accordingly, it was acclaimed as the centre of worship for its three services per year and it welcomed back old friends with open arms. The atmosphere was the same as before, nothing had changed and those resolute supporters of the new chapel changed their allegiance back to the old one.

The three services are held on the first Sunday in May, the fourth Sunday in June and the third Sunday in August. I was privileged to attend the May service in 1993, when I saw the chapel's old-fashioned beauty and goodness. Even though it was a warm day, a roaring fire was blazing in the fireplace and the older ladies of the congregation wore their best coats, hats and gloves, in deference to the occasion. In 1991, the old chapel was given a new lease of life, and the Parish Council implemented plans to extend the graveyard.

In December 1993, it was decided to hold a Carol Service in addition to the other three services. This was such a success that it is now hoped to hold one every year. On Sunday 18th December, 1994, I attended the second Carol Service. I arrived early, to watch the chapel being prepared. The Blackburn and Darwen Band arrived and arranged their members and instruments below the pulpit. The Tilley lamps were primed, lit and then hoisted to their positions hanging from the ceiling. Caring hands placed candles in jars on the windowsills. There was holly and mistletoe, ivy and poinsettias, evergreens and shining woodwork. The whole room reflected glory.The fire burned brightly; old people, who'd attended the chapel many years ago, exchanged fond greetings and memories. I watched in wonder as the tiny building filled to capacity, marvelling at the atmosphere and the wonderful dedication of its tiny band of workers, who had brought their dream to fruition. When everyone was in place it was 'standing room only', the band began the first carol and the service commenced. The lamps hissed gently, the candles glowed and, as darkness descended over the little chapel on the moors, it was like a true Dickensian Christmas. The beauty of the setting and the occasion overwhelmed everyone. Afterwards, coffee and mince pies were served in the little vestry adjoining the chapel and there was a chance for people to exchange greetings and good wishes. The trustees of the chapel and their dedicated band of workers are to be applauded for their efforts in keeping this tradition, and the chapel, alive.

What of the future? One can only hope that future generations will cherish and care for Pickup Bank Old Chapel as well as their forbears have done, and that it will serve a useful purpose for many years to come. As I drove away from the tiny chapel, the candle lights were twinkling in the windows and the first few flakes of snow added to the beauty of the scene. Pickup Bank Congregational Chapel has stood the test of time for almost two centuries and has not lost any of its attraction and charm. It still means so much to so many people and I hope that that same spirit of love and care will exist well into the twenty-first century, remaining part of Pickup Bank's heritage for many years to come.

ALFRED ERNEST TYSOE, a Lanky typhoon and whirlwind

Alfred Ernest Tysoe was born in Padiham, near Burnley, on 21st March 1874. He died, aged 27, in Marton, Blackpool, on 26th October 1901. During Alfred's short stay on earth, he enjoyed a meteoric rise to fame in the world of athletics. Had this lad been running in this day and age, I have no doubts that he would have been a very rich man indeed; as it was, he was born in the age of true amateur sportsmen and his monetary rewards were little. There was no shortage of fortune in the shape of medals.

As a young boy he had moved from Padiham with his parents to a farm in upper Wyresdale, near Dolphinholme, where he relished the space and fresh air. At school he was encouraged to take up fell running. This was to prove very beneficial, he developed very strong legs and powerful lungs, the requisites of any running champion.

A member of the Lancaster-based Skerton Harriers observed Alfred on his jaunts around the fellsides and suggested to the boy that he had a future in athletics. He felt that the lad ought to join the Harriers. This he did and from that moment he was on the fast track to glory.

To the First Division

Alfred quickly learnt the arts of a runner, and within a very short space of time he was beating seasoned runners, some of whom had ten or more years of competition under their belt. The young lad won races over many distances, from 100 yards to ten miles. Whilst still running in the colours of Skerton Harriers, he won the 1896 Northern Counties Amateur Championship at Lancaster. This win made him the target of the bigger clubs. He was approached by several and decided to join Salford Harriers.

A True British Champ

This move was a major step in Alfred's career. Here he had better facilities. He moved up a gear and entered more races against the cream of English athletes. During his first year with Salford he won the National 1000 yards race and the premium mile event. The following year, 1898, he did the feat again, and for good measure added the half mile to his tally. In the next year he again got the hat trick over the same distances. For good measure he won the mile and half mile titles the following season; for some obscure reason the 1000 yards was declared void; in 1900 he entered all three races, and once again won all three first prizes. Mention must also be made of two singularly good results in the English championships when he won the one mile, and the ten mile events against some of the world's best atheletes.

His best result of 1899 was the thrashing he handed out to that mercurial runner, the Reverend E. E. Lutyens, over the half mile distance which Tysoe covered in the remarkable time of 1 minute 58.35 seconds. Lutyens was left in his wake, no doubt as astonished as his supporters who were there in force waiting to cheer his expected victory. The cheers on that day however were for Tysoe.

The Best Has Yet to Come

Better was yet to come for a boy who was rapidly becoming a force in world athletics circles. In the 1900 English championship, which was open to all comers, he was ranged against the best half milers in the world: the field included the almost invincible American runner, J. C. Cregan. Although Cregan got off to a flyer, within a very short space of time the lanky, fair-haired Tysoe had overtaken him to fly home in 1 minute 57.4 seconds. Cregan did not like, or expect, to be beaten by Tysoe; he suggested that the 'Limey' was lucky, and that should they ever meet again then he would wipe the floor with him.

The event which fate had decreed would match these two runners over the 800 distance was at the Olympic Games in Paris. This event was quite unique, because for the first time at any international event, amateurs were to be competing head to head with the professional athletes. Several of the field were running for money; Tysoe was running for Britain and glory.

John Cregan was the world champion, a big powerful man who was determined to put this upstart Tysoe in his place. In the event it was the champion who was shown his place, second to our hero, who cantered home in the time of 2 minutes 1.2 seconds, Cregan some way behind came in at 2 minutes 3 seconds. The third man was the American professional David Hall. This time Cregan accepted defeat with honour and shook the victor's hand at the medal ceremony.

At the Olympic meeting, Charles Bennet, of Finchley Harriers, had won the 1500 metre event for Great Britain. It was suggested that he and Tysoe should run against each other to prove just who was the better. The race took place in Manchester in front of a crowd of several thousand eager and expectant spectators, each of whom had their favourite. The distance chosen was three quarters of a mile. Tysoe won in 3 minutes 13 seconds, leaving Bennet twenty yards adrift.

Sadly, this proved to be the last major event Alfred participated in. Almost from that moment his health began to fail; he was never to recover.

By now his parents were living in Blackpool, and his doctor suggested he went to live with them as the sea air may benefit him. This was not to be the case. Soon after arriving at his parents home he fell dangerously ill. Two eminent doctors examined him, the diagnosis was very severe, meningitis. This on top of the bronchial pneumonia afflicting him was to prove fatal. As arrangements were being made to move Tysoe to a sanitorium at Grange-over-Sands, he collapsed and expired.

A. E. Tysoe won over a hundred first prizes at all levels and over many distances. He also won twenty two national and local championship medals, plus the Olympic gold medal. This medal may well have been the very first Olympic gold won by anyone from the Red Rose county!

He lies at rest today in the Layton cemetery in Blackpool, his last lap has been run, the last prize collected, the ringing cheers which greeted his every win are now but echoes on the wind.

Yes! Alfred has gone from our midst, but he bequeathed his native county a golden legacy which deserves to live on forever.

LOVELY LANCASHIRE LETTERS

In Victorian and Edwardian times, firms and companies sent out letters and invoices on notepaper headed not only by their name but also embellished with drawings illustrating their product, premises or trade mark. Here are a few examples:

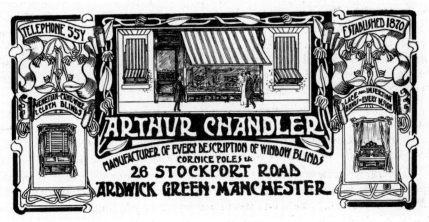

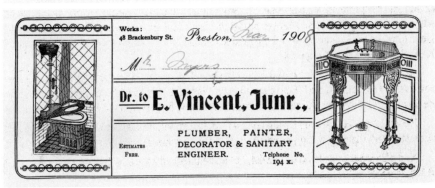

SOME LANCASHIRE PEN-NAMES

A computer has replaced the card index system on which, for some years, I recorded the pen-names used by authors with a Lancashire connection. By that I mean that he/she lived or was born in our county, or wrote in its dialect. 325 writers and names are in the index.

Here are a few notes printed out after being keyed in following information being passed to me. If you have anything to say, or want information on Lancashire authors and the pen-names they use(d), please write to me c/o the publisher of this book.

The most prolific user of pen-names we have produced was **John Russell Fearn**, a science fiction writer - best known as Vargo Statten - from Worsley and the Fylde, with at least twenty names - *John Cotton, Poulton Cross, Thornton Ayre* amongst them. Next is **Charles Allen Clarke**, who lived in Bolton and Blackpool, with fourteen to his name - *Teddy Ashton* being his best known.

Of longest standing perhaps is *Tim Bobbin*, used by **John Collier** (1708-86) of Milnrow. Three pubs in Lancashire and one in London carry his 'Name'.

A Lancashire Lad had been used by several writers, amongst them **Mr. Donaldson** from Haslingden and **John Whittaker**, another Rossendalian. **Mrs. E. J. Bellasis** (from where?) called herself *A Lancashire Lady* when penning.

Some famous names appear in my collection - *Leslie Charteris*, creator of 'The Saint' was called **Leslie Charteris Bowyer Yin** when at Rossall School. **Mrs. Gaskell**, author of Mary Barton and North and South, also wrote as *Cotton Mather Mills*. **Walter de la Mare** dreamed of daffodils in the far North of the county and also wrote as *Walter Ramal*.

Humour abounds; *Th'owd Fossil* was **Jane Fitton**, the wife of **Sam**, who was also *Peter Pike, Billy Blob* and *Sally Butter'orth*. **Alfred Pearce** and his wife **Edith**, from Droylsden, founding stalwarts of the Lancashire Authors Association, wrote as *Lord and Lady Knowswho*.

I record names given to writers by other people - **Samuel Bamford** was *The Bard of Middleton*; **James Conway** was *The Policeman Poet*; **Henry Houlding** was *The Pendle Laurate* and Preston-born **Robert Service** was *The Klondike Poet*.

Many queries exist. Where did **John Scholes** (*Abram o'Flup*) and **Harold Wynch** (*Hal Hilyard*) hail from? Who was Rossendale's *Obadiah Perriwinkle*, Liverpool's *Sam Dicky*, Accrington's *Amicus*? Who was *Matty Hari, Jone o'Jeffries, Owd Shuttle, Penelope North, O.C.K., C.F.C.* and *J.F.B.*?

Right: William Harrison would certainly recognise this 19th Century view of the Hob Inn at Bamber Bridge, twixt Preston and Chorley, though today's drinkers and diners at this old coaching house on the A6 road might have difficulty.

ONE OF THE OLD BRIGADE: WILLIAM HARRISON

Owd Bill Harrison was described by the *'Chorley Guardian'* as a *"peculiar and eccentric character"*. How true, for this one-time innkeeper, butcher and horse dealer was a one-off. A year before he died, aged 82 years, he sent out many copies of the following letter to friends throughout the country. His funeral arrangements were carried out almost to the letter - traps were allowed as well as carts, and the event took place on a Monday.

I, William Harrison, senior, of Bolton Street, Chorley,voluntarily and of my own free will, make the following arrangements for my funeral, namely:- That my coffin be made of oak, and furnished with brass handles and brassplate, but no black to be allowed on; that my Crooked Stick be put in my coffin beside my right hand; that I be interred in Blackrod Parish Church Yard; that if possible the funeral to be on a Sunday; that the hearse shall have glass sides but no feathers nor plumes, and to be drawn by four grey horses; that no mourning coach be allowed to follow, but shandrys and carts may be used; that neither sons nor daughters, nor any relatives or friends, to follow me to my grave in black clothes; that my relations and friends immediately after the funeral must get something to eat and drink at Blackrod, to be provided at Robert Harrison's; that 10lbs of sweets be given to children at Blackrod; that when all relatives and friends who have attended the funeral have returned to Chorley, all must have as much refreshment as they can eat and drink; and that 20lbs of sweets be given to my grandchildren at Chorley. All these arrangements I request to be faithfully carried out by my executors at my death.

Dated this 30th day of May, 1884

William Harrison his mark

Witness Robert Harrison

GREATER LANCASHIRE

The **Friends of Real Lancashire, FORL**, is an organisation devoted to the restoration of our county's name throughout its whole extent, irrespective of which council administers the area. The organisation is nobbut a youngster, but has chalked up some achievements.

'*The Lancastrian*' is the annual FORL magazine. A recent issue contained:- a piece on Pilkington Glass Company getting paid just one red rose for leasing land to the Grange Park Golf Club; Garston having a Chester Street in which there was a murder in the early years of this century, whereupon the name was changed to Chesterton Street; a map showing one hundred miles of inland waterways in Lancashire; the refusal of Lancashire County Cricket Club, whose home is in Stretford, to use words other than Lancashire in their address or title; and how the BBC, replying to a letter from FORL said, *"Our policy is to refer to places according to their modern boundaries"*. When will they start to listen to their listeners, who are telling them that they want to have the '*L-word*' restored? You can tell the Editor of News & Current Affairs, BBC North, Oxford Road, Manchester M60 1SJ, LANCASHIRE, of your views.

A year's subscription to FORL costs £4 (Family £6, Corporate £5). The Membership Secretary is Mrs. Janet Brooks, Oaklea Cottage, Grange-over-Sands, LA11 6RB.

The Friends have declared that 27th November each year will be **LANCASHIRE DAY**. This was the date on which, in 1295 , Lancashire's first representatives attended the king's court, the then equivalent of Parliament. The first Lancashire Day was held in 1996. Town criers proclaimed it and rhymsters ranted about it. One was penned by Ron Williams of Saddleworth, the first verse goes:

LANCISHER DAY

Lancisher Day; t' 27th o' November
A bran new date fer uz to remember
So let uz sheawt it eawt reet leawd
It's a day to mak loyal Lankys preawd.
So get thi 'hot pots' into th'oon
On November neets yon is a boon
Wi' t'black pudd's simmerin' i' th'pon
Un honeycomb thripe - wi onions on
Som' Lancisher cheyse, wi a Blackpool roll
Should mak thi dinner table whole
Wi cakes fro' Eccles - ur Chorley i'deed
Theau'll 'ave a gradely Lanky feed.